Celtic Britain

Celtic Britain

Text and Photography by Homer Sykes

CASSELLPAPERBACKS

For my daughter Tallulabelle, Wiggly, Gossamer, Bluebell,
and all our friends at the bottom of the garden.

First published in the United Kingdom in 1997 by
Weidenfeld & Nicolson Ltd

This paperback edition first published in 2001 by
Cassell Paperbacks, Cassell & Co
Wellington House, 125 Strand
London, WC2R 0BB

Text and photographs copyright © Homer Sykes, 1997

Distributed in the United States of America by
Sterling Publishing Co., Inc.
387 Park Avenue South,
New York, NY 10016-8810

Designed By Paul Cooper
Edited By Caroline Earle
Map by Jennie Dooge

A CIP catalogue record for this book is available
from the British Library

ISBN 1-84188-150-3

Printed and bound in Italy

Title page: Men-an-Tol, near Morvah, Cornwall

CONTENTS

Page number references to map opposite

Outer Hebrides

Stornoway
27

Peterhead

Inverness

Aberdeen
89

Orkney Islands
110

Shetland Islands
18
111
61

98, 99, 100, 101

Oban
78
Dundee
Perth
62

102, 104, 105, 106
103
47
79
39, 40, 41

Glasgow
147
Edinburgh
63

Berwick-upon-Tweed
109
108
88

20, 21, 76, 77, 96
Isle of Arran

Campbeltown

Newcastle

97

Carlisle

24
46

Middlesbrough

Blackpool
151
Hull

Manchester

Liverpool

S.W. England

132

72, 127
73
145
Exeter

80, 91
92
22, 25
153
26, 93

48, 49, 86

23, 70
74
71
Truro

2, 75
52, 149
126

60, 107
130, 131,
144

66, 67
124, 125
87
44, 45
128
123
137
64, 135
Caernarfon
68
122
129
148
65
136
113
59

133
Nottingham

Peterborough

Great Yarmouth

Cambridge

Birmingham

Stratford-upon-Avon

Aberystwyth
32
146

14, 120
19
57, 56
Cardigan
28, 29
Swansea
118
119

42, 43
38
58

142, 143
33
150
Oxford

London

114, 115, 116, 117
112
Cardiff
138
69
50
90
94, 95

8, 34, 35, 36, 37, 51

30, 31, 152

Bath

Dover

121
134

Brighton

Exeter

Bournemouth

Truro

INTRODUCTION

Silbury Hill
Nr Avebury, Wiltshire

Silbury Hill is one of the wonders of prehistoric Celtic Britain. It is the tallest prehistoric mound in Europe and is 130 feet in height and 100 feet across its flat top. Totally unique, almost nothing is known about it, though surely it must form part of the Avebury prehistoric complex. Perhaps it was a symbol of authority, a place from where a great leader could look down on his people.

Archaeologists have discovered that it was built in three stages. Originally a normal-sized, barrow-shaped mound was made and enclosed with a ring of wooden poles. Then at a later date chalk excavated from the surrounding ditch was added to cover the mound. This smaller enterprise was abandoned, the ditch was filled and the present mound was built in a series of chalk steps. It took about 18 million hours to construct, during the late Neolithic and the early Bronze Age periods.

Legends associated with Silbury Hill suggest that it was the burial mound for the great King Sil and his fabled golden horse. However, there have been three excavations over the last 200 years and nothing has been found.

Celt is a generic name which means different things to different people. To define Celtic Britain, I have attempted to blur and blend some of the traditionally held views regarding its meaning. The landscapes in Celtic Britain include sites and places that, from a strict archaeological and historical perspective, are pre-Celtic, i.e. pre-Iron Age. Leading authorities have argued that the Iron Age Celts had their roots in the Bronze Age culture, and that they in turn were the lineal descendants of Neolithic man. Celticization was a gradual process and the indigenous people of Britain, cut off from their neighbours by the English Channel, developed in their own way over millennia. Many of these landscapes are situated in a geographical area of Britain that has a Celtic oral tradition, and often they are associated through myth and legend with Celtic tradition. This book on Celtic Britain touches the late Neolithic period, spans the Bronze and the Iron Age, as well as the period after the Roman withdrawal from Britain – traditionally called the 'Dark Ages' – including the mysteries of the Arthurian legend, as well as the coming of Christianity. During the medieval period craftsmen perpetuated a Celtic tradition by incorporating carvings of enigmatic pagan deities into the detailing and decoration of Christian churches. Finally, the Neodruidic revival, and contemporary Druids are touched upon. Celtic Britain is shown to be still vibrant, and places are visited where pagan Celtic traditions are still performed.

Over 6,000 years are covered in this volume, and as such I have only lightly scraped the surface of our Celtic past. The Neolithic and Bronze Age people of Britain were farmers, hunters and fisherman. They buried their great leaders in massive stone constructions and the skeletons of these tombs are now often all that remain. In Wales, Careg Samson, for example, is a short walk along the coastal path from the unspoilt fishing village of Abercastle. Local fishing boats sway in the calm shelter of the bay, piles of lobster pots are stacked on the quay. The coastal path and meadow leading to Careg Samson in May is ablaze with wild flowers: thrift, kingcups and buttercups, white and pink campions, archangel, spring squill, primroses and stonecrop. This enormous and beautiful cromlech ('curved stone' in English) probably takes its name from a popular local Celtic saint, Samson. Nearby is Pentre Ifan – which was once known as Arthur's Quoit – probably the most famous prehistoric burial site in Wales. Over the centuries innumerable folktales and legends have become associated with this site, and according to one tale it was a place of Druidic sacrifice. Neither of these two sites strictly fit into the historical context of Celtic Britain but they are both without doubt part of the rich and prehistoric tapestry of our Celtic landscape. The Bronze Age people buried their dead in barrows: huge, round mausoleums which, when completed, were covered with earth to form a shape like an upturned cup. Over the thousands of years since they were constructed they have often been ploughed down, and so all too often are seen today as small round hillocks in a ploughed field. They are visually distinct from the commercial crops that grow there, since grass and weeds grow on them producing a different colour. Where they have been preserved, often by accident, they are tall and massive. Just north of the prosperous market town of Marlborough are the three Ogbourne villages – Maizey, St Andrew and St George. At first glance, there is nothing particularly unusual about them: horses flick their tails and canter with their young in the neatly fenced fields, young children are collected from nearby schools by nannies, and on Sunday the church is full of prosperous villagers. These villages flourish, they are small, conservative and exclusive. However, at Ogbourne St Andrew all is not as it might at first seem. Built within the churchyard is a large, and now tree-covered pagan, Bronze Age round barrow. When the first church was constructed here, the words spoken by Pope Gregory decades earlier might well have rung in the ears of the congregation. He is reported to have said in AD 601 to Abbot Mellitus that he had dwelt on the conversion of the Celts and decided that their pagan deities and temples should not be dismantled, but rather purified with holy water and Christian altars. These should be set up to take their place in surroundings which were familiar, he surmised, so that the Celts would embrace the new faith, Christianity, more readily. There are numerous examples throughout Britain's Celtic landscape that illustrate the continuity from one pagan place of worship to a Christian one.

The first prehistoric Celts constructed enigmatic and mysterious stone circles, and erected huge single stones known as menhirs. These were sometimes single 'marking' stones; Bordastubble Standing Stone in the Shetland Islands is one such menhir. At other times these stones formed part of a grouping – for example, the stone rows that are to be found on Dartmoor. Wherever there were communities of people, often extending only to a few families, they built stone circles and erected great stone totem poles. According to Professor Alexander Thom and his son Archie, leading authorities in this field, some of these stones were designed to be aligned to the sun, the moon and the stars. Loch Buie Stone Circle on the Isle of Mull, off the west coast of Scotland, is an example of a small and nearly perfectly preserved stone circle. It is situated on the only area of flat, fertile land on the south coast of a very mountainous, and probably in prehistoric times inhospitable, island. The community here could never have been large, for the land would not have supported more than a few extended families. Nevertheless, the importance of their religious beliefs was such that these people were able to construct this circle, and shape and add at least two large stone outlyers, which are believed to have been aligned to the midwinter sunset. This was perhaps a meeting place of some special significance to prehistoric people, who may well have come from the mainland across the Firth of Lorne at significant times of the year for worship and ritual magic. These Stone Age sites were once scattered throughout the British landscape. Now only relatively few remain, principally because of their remote locations where the landscape has changed surprisingly little over 6,000 years.

Four thousand years after this period of British prehistory, Greek and Roman scholars were to write about the Celts with completely differing views on who they were. The first written reference to these people is by the classical Greek scholar Hecataeus of Miletus, who alluded to the Keltoi in 500 BC, and described the Celts as tall, blond and with aquiline features. The Roman scholar Herodotus, who mentions them in his *Histories*, describes the Celts as being small and fierce with dark complexions. These pre-Christian Celtic tribes dominated Europe and occupied land from Spain in the south to Ireland in the west, and on through to what is now Eastern Europe. From the end of what is traditionally called the Bronze Age through to the beginning of the Dark Ages, these Iron Age warriors controlled continental Europe. Judging from the abundance of hillforts stretching across Europe and Britain these were troubled times. They were a warlike, ferocious, tribal people, who daubed their bodies in woad and went into combat (according to some accounts) naked. Some of these hillforts were much more; they were the first towns. Traprain Law, a few miles south-east of Edinburgh, was during the Iron Age the capital of a tribe called the Votadini, who eventually moved their capital to Edinburgh (Dun Edin). These Iron Age Celts were able to support non food producers since the wealth that they created was enormous – the treasures that were buried with their leaders and the legends that were associated with them are evidence of this. Silbury Hill, which is part of the Avebury complex, is reputed to hold not only the body of the great King Sil, but a life-sized gold statue of his horse!

Their society comprised kings, a warrior-nobility, artisans, and teachers. The teachers were their religious leaders – the Druids. Lamentably their tradition was oral, they had no written language, therefore it is impossible to know if they actually thought of themselves as Celts. We have to depend on archaeological proof, inscriptions found on Iron Age coins and what little linguistic evidence still remains in the form of place names. The Wrekin Hillfort is one such place that has, with little change, kept its Celtic name:

Uriconion. We know that by the first century BC the Celtic language was spoken in various forms throughout Britain, Gaul, Northern Italy, Spain, and Central and Eastern Europe. There is no evidence that these warring tribes, who so dominated and fought their way across continental Europe, ever invaded Britain *en masse* – unlike their successors, the Romans, whose invasion of Britain in AD 43 marks the end of the Iron Age period. To the lay reader it is easy to assume that the dates scholars give the various periods in British history are hard and fast. Of course this is not the case. The changes from one form of society, their beliefs and the buildings they constructed, the tools and daily implements that they used all took hundreds of years to stylistically develop. In many cases the cultural change that took place as a result of these new Roman influences had hardly begun before the Romans withdrew from Britain 500 years later. Parts of Cornwall, Wales and Scotland were never successfully invaded and Romanized. The Romans found it difficult to reach North-West Wales and Anglesey, the centres of Druidism, since they had to contend with the well-organized Silures in the south of the country and the Ordovices in the north. Having tried without success on two occasions to invade what we now know as Scotland, the Romans left that part of Celtic Britain to the indigenous tribes, amongst others, the Scots and Picts. The Roman Emperor Hadrian built his wall across the country at its narrowest point to keep the troublesome and unconquerable Picts out of Roman Britain.

When the Roman armies withdrew, Britain entered what historians used to call the Dark Ages. This was a period when Britain was being invaded by warring pagan tribes from continental Europe, who were undoubtedly attacking and driving the indigenous Celtic peoples of Britain to the extremities of the country. This book follows the flight of those Celtic Britons to the West Country, to Cornwall, Devon and Somerset, and to Wales and up into Scotland, where evangelizing Celtic holy men and women, who had sailed at great personal risk to these shores to convert their pagan neighbours, were beginning to have success. Some of these holy men and women set up baptisteries, others lived as hermits, while a few formed Celtic Christian communities that eventually became centres of learning. They proved very popular and had a massive following, for example, the religious centre at Llanwit Major in Wales. A few of these holy men – such as St David, who gives his name to the smallest city in Britain and is the patron saint of Wales – are still remembered as national figures. While in Cornwall it seems that almost every granite village is named after a Celtic saint: Tudy, Levan, Endellion, Germoe and Kew to name but five. Today these Celtic saints are not widely known outside their immediate parish. However, they most certainly have left an indelible mark on Celtic Cornwall.

The Dark Ages are also of course associated with the romantic and heroic British leader, a saviour of the Celtic people, a man called Arthur, around whom numerous and well-loved legends and interrelating folktales have developed. There is much conjecture as to the whereabouts of the places in Arthurian legend, and if indeed they actually ever existed. Scholars have, however, researched and pinpointed where some of the places mentioned can be found. For example, King Arthur's castle is popularly thought to have been at Tintagel in Cornwall. The Tudor antiquarian John Leyland, writing many years after Arthur's time, speculated that it was at South Cadbury. He based this theory on the romantic French addition to the stories written seven centuries after Arthur, that Camelot was the court of King Arthur. The village names were similar, and villagers of South Cadbury were intent on claiming their part in what had become a popular legend. Subsequently, twentieth-century archaeologists have carried out extensive and careful excavation here. South Cadbury Castle is Iron Age, though it was extensively reused at a later date; the time and new findings fit perfectly with that of Arthur. South Cadbury may well have been the stronghold from which he went out and fought the Saxons. Both these and other sites will be explored in this book on Celtic Britain. Lastly this volume takes the reader to contemporary Celtic Britain, a Britain that for a few people still has a pagan Celtic tradition. Throughout the summer months in nearly every country village, and in a good many towns as well, it is impossible not to notice teams of quaintly dressed men in 'olde English' dress, bedecked with ribbons and with bells jangling, stomping and leaping, handkerchiefs waving. They are performing a traditional English country dance. These Morris dances had by the end of the last century almost died out, but were revived almost single-handedly by Cecil Sharp, a folklorist, and they are just one example of a popular country pursuit that has its origins in pagan Celtic tradition and can be associated with the Celtic sun god, Belenus.

NEOLITHIC AND BRONZE AGE

Pentre Ifan Cromlech
Nr Nevern, Pembrokeshire

Of the many prehistoric monuments in Wales, Pentre Ifan is probably the best known. Looking out across the Pembrokeshire National Park, three huge uprights support a delicately balanced, enormous, sixteen-feet-long capstone. This burial chamber was built by prehistoric man 4,000 years ago. Up to fifty tribesmen and women, along with their chiefs, were buried here over many years. Excavation has shown that this prehistoric 'cathedral' was laid out in an oval pit. Once sealed, the long barrow was covered with a huge mound of earth 130 feet long and retained by a dry stone and timber wall, which has now been eroded away.

Also known as Arthur's Quoit, the site of this cromlech (or curved stone) according to legend has been associated with Druidic sacrificial rites. Samson's Quoit and Llech y Drybedd are of the same period and are nearby, as is Nevern Church, famous for its celtic cross.

Celtic Britain is scattered with numerous Neolithic and Bronze Age sites, virtually all of them in remote corners of the country and, by their very nature, small in comparison to the two most spectacular sites from this period: Stonehenge and Avebury. These sites dominate and excite the imagination, not only of the specialists but, more importantly, of ordinary Britons, and both are easily accessible. In Scotland the two major sites included in this volume are the Machrie Moor Standing Stones on the Isle of Arran and the Callanish Standing Stones in the Outer Hebrides.

I asked a farmer how long it would take me to walk to Carn Menyn and Beddarthur. 'About an hour, it depends on how fast you walk,' he said. Looking up at the rain-heavy, dark, brooding clouds, optimistically I said. 'And will the weather be fine?' 'Oh yes, you might have a shower, half the cows are sitting down.' An hour later, past thick, ruined earth and stone walls that make the ancient Celtic field pattern seeming almost as old as the stones themselves, I arrived at Carn Menyn and its frost-shattered, boulder-strewn, lower slopes. These could have been the playbricks of some giant's child. But they are not; they are the bluestones that prehistoric man collected and shaped. Eighty of them, each weighing about four tons, were then transported to the sea by pushing and dragging on wooden rollers with teams of oxen, where they were slung between boats and slowly sailed around the coast of Wales and up the River Severn. Only then to be dragged and rolled once more across wood- and shrub-covered countryside, eventually reaching Salisbury Plain, where they were, according to the late Professor Richard Atkinson, the leading authority on Stonehenge, erected in the second phase of construction within the great Neolithic henge – a ditch and earth bank.

These bluestones are known to exist only in two places: the Prescelly Mountains of west Wales and in southern Ireland. When cut and wet they take on a blue hue, which, quite possibly to prehistoric man, had some special religious and magical significance that we no longer understand. If this is not the case, then why did these prehistoric Celts not use more readily available stone quarries? The great tribal leaders of the Bronze Age were powerful and fabulously rich, as testified by the finds that accompanied them in their round barrow mausoleums that dot the landscape. They must have commanded unwavering loyalty in order to have organized and directed the teams of men and women in the building of their huge and astronomically precisely designed places of worship. The continuity of purpose is staggering: Stonehenge was built in three stages, often hundreds of years between each stage, and in all it took nearly a thousand years to evolve.

The prehistoric site at Avebury, like its better known neighbour Stonehenge, is a vast monument that now encompasses part of the village of Avebury. The enormous henge alone is estimated to have taken more than 1,500,000 man hours to dig out, an estimated 3,900,000 cubic feet of chalk, dug with picks made from antlers, and shoulder blades used as shovels. The chalk was levered out of the ground, shovelled into crude baskets and then hauled out and deposited to form a bank. Huge local sarsen stones were then edged into place, the largest weighing nearly fifty tons. Teams of skilled men manoeuvring these great boulders then levered them up, before dropping and sliding them into predug holes. The colossal sarsen stones form the largest stone circle in Britain and within this great circle are two smaller ones. Leading south from this monumental temple is the West Kennet Avenue, which meanders to a small concentric circle known as The Sanctuary. Leading westward from the great circle is the now-forgotten Beckhampton Avenue. Only two stones, known as Adam and Eve, are still extant, all the others have long since been destroyed. These avenues were surely a prehistoric processional route, used on great ceremonial occasions. A mile to the south is Silbury Hill, a huge, fascinating, prehistoric flat-topped earth mound. Its purpose has never been fathomed. Could it have been where great Celtic tribal leaders gathered with their courts to survey their subjects on auspicious occasions prior to processing to the Avebury Temple? In all, this monument complex may well have taken 500 men, working for several months of each year after the harvest, at least fifty years to finish.

While waiting for the roll-on-roll-off ferry from Lochranza to Claonaig, I watched a thousand white horses rise and break; two gulls facing the howling Atlantic winds hovered and then dived arrow-like for their lunch. I marvelled at their speed and optimism. The ferryman told me that we would be sailing late. The storm was blowing through, though the sea looked fine, the swell was high and it would be very difficult for the ferry to land safely at Claonaig for the return journey to Arran. I was heading for Machrie Moor on the west coast, one of the most enigmatic prehistoric Celtic sites in Britain. We left precisely on the adjusted time and some twenty minutes later I had my first glimpse of Arran – huge, rounded, mist-covered mountains dominated the horizon, while below lush green fields and white, crisply painted crofters' cottages framed in black dotted the landscape. Machrie Moor was once a great Celtic tribal centre. Here are the remains of numerous stone circles. Four large stones from two circles dominate, and they are pitted and grooved due to the passage of time. Other circles are made from smaller, rounded boulders. Archaeologists have revealed these stone circles, but beneath the thick spongy layer of peat one cannot help but wonder if other circles remain hidden. This alluvial and arable land was fertile, the sea plentiful and numerous families farmed and lived here. Then towards the end of the Bronze Age the climate began to deteriorate significantly, and this, combined with poor farming methodology, led to the site being deserted. In the Lake District there are stone circles dating from a similar and earlier periods. Nearly all are situated on low, fertile land. There is one exception – the circles at Brats Hill. They are reached after a steep and an exhilarating climb, and the views of scenery unaltered by modern man are spectacular. On this high, windy, and often rain-drenched plateau it is difficult to imagine prehistoric families farming and living in relative comfort. But they did. Judging by the number of circles and burial sites, this was a prosperous community. With the climatic change they, too, would have moved further down into the valley, abandoning their temples, burial sites and homes. Other sites over the thousands of years may well have been abandoned due to inclement weather and a population developing different cultural traditions. There is ample evidence to illustrate the development from Stone to Bronze Age sites. In turn, these sites were adapted for use in the Iron Age, and so on through the centuries. Jarlshof in the Shetland Islands was only rediscovered relatively recently, having been buried beneath a blanket of sand for hundreds of years. This is a site that until being finally abandoned in the medieval period had been continually occupied, probably longer than any other place in Britain. Successive layers of sand preserved different periods of building production. The first inhabitants belonged to the late Neolithic period. Bronze Age man then took over, and in turn Picts, who were followed by Norse invaders, in time giving way to a medieval farm.

Within the stone circle at Ysbyty Cynfyn, near Devil's Bridge, which according to local folklore 'was once the haunt of the Druids', an early Christian settlement was established. Later a church was dedicated to St John the Baptist. Only four of the original great stones that made up what once must have been a massive circle still remain, incorporated into the retaining wall of the churchyard. The continuation and Christianization of pagan places is clearly demonstrated here. Interestingly for this tiny remote hamlet in Welsh-speaking Wales, a sign on the board outside the church announces: 'All services will be held in English unless otherwise specified.'

Bordastubble Standing Stone
Burragarth, Unst, Shetland

Bordastubble Standing Stone is situated a mile from the roll-on-roll-off ferry that carries you from Gutcher on the island of Yell, across Bluemull Sound to the most northerly island in the Shetlands, Unst. Tilting precariously and standing nearly twelve feet tall, this huge, lichen-covered monolith has a circumference of over eight feet. At its base, several sizeable packing stones keep it just about upright. It is the largest monolith in the Shetland Islands. Like many standing stones of the late Neolithic and early Bronze Age period, it is impossible to say with any accuracy why it was erected. Possibly to define a boundary, perhaps to mark a grave, or it may well once have been part of a network of other monoliths on the island. However, its significance, which may have been ritual and has now been lost during the passage of the intervening centuries, must have been such that it has stood unmoved for more than 4,000 years.

Llech y Drybedd
Nr Molygrove, Pembrokeshire

Llech y Drybedd translates into English as the 'Stone of the Three Graves'. It is an extremely impressive squat burial chamber and it is all that remains of a prehistoric long barrow. It would have once been covered with a huge mound of earth, which has been eroded away over a period of several thousand years since its construction. This is probably the last resting place of some great Neolithic leader. Not as well known as Pentre Ifan just a few miles away, it can be found situated up a rough farm track immediately west of Penlan Farm, near the picturesque village of Molygrove. According to legend, this enormous stone was tossed by Samson from the summit of Mount Carningli. There is confusion as to which Samson this could have been. Samson whose heroic strength is recorded in early Biblical tales? Or St Samson whose name is associated with numerous prehistoric sites in west Wales?

Machrie Moor
Nr Blackwaterfoot, Isle of Arran, North Ayrshire

All that now remains of two large circles are the four huge standing stones on Machrie Moor. Mysteriously grooved, this sandstone megalith was once part of a nine-stone circle. Excavated more than a hundred years ago, two cists (stone burial chambers) were found at its centre. One contained the skull of a young man accompanied by two flint arrow heads. Nearby are three large sandstone pillars and a split circular slab. Once thought to be a sacrificial altar stone, where razor-sharp daggers may have been plunged into Celtic cult victims, recent investigation suggests it is a broken millstone pushed together and placed here years ago.

When these stone circles were erected during the later years of the Neolithic period and during the early Bronze Age, the climate of Arran was much kinder than it is now. This moor was a fertile pasture capable of supporting a community of farmers and fishermen. Machrie Moor was a unique cult centre. There are at least four chambered tombs, five cairns, four other stone circles and three standing stones. Towards the end of the Bronze Age the site was finally abandoned. Now covered with a blanket of boggy peat, one can only speculate as to the megalithic mysteries still to be uncovered.

Stone Row
Merrivale, Dartmoor, Devon

On Dartmoor there are in the region of sixty recorded enigmatic stone rows, more here than anywhere else in Britain. Some of these rows are very long, others are short, some double, and some even triple. Most often they end at a stone cist. In nearly every case, the rows have been to some extent robbed of their stones. The stone row on Long Ash Hill near Merrivale is unique on Dartmoor, comprising two nearly parallel double rows of stones thirty yards apart. At one end is a stone cist, at the other a group of hut circles. No one knows the meaning of these rows, but it is generally thought that since so many of them end at a cist that they were some sort of processional route leading up to a place of burial of a great Bronze Age clan leader.

Zennor Quoit
Zennor, Cornwall

Zennor Quoit stands on a high ridge above the diminutive village that gave the quoit its name. This huge Neolithic tomb has five massive upright slabs supporting an enormous nine and a half ton cap stone. This has now slipped, thanks to a farmer who wanted to break up and dismantle the tomb so that he could use the material to built a cattle shed.

The quoit was saved by the vicar of Zennor, a member of the Borlase family. A report in the *Cornish Telegraph* in 1861 reads: 'On hearing of the vandalism the Vicar set out, offering the farmer five shilling not to proceed with the cattle shed.' His offer was accepted, but unfortunately much damage had already been done.

Excavations have not been particularly successful, the tomb having been subjected to treasure seekers over the years. However, some Neolithic and Bronze Age fragments of pottery, flints, bones and a perforated whetstone have been found, indicating that the site was in use up until at least 1,500 BC.

Brats Hill Stone Circle
Nr Boot, Cumbria

Unlike most prehistoric stone circles that are constructed on low-lying ground, the group of five circles at Brats Hill are a two-mile hike up Gill Bank from the tiny hamlet of Boot in Eskdale. This mysterious burial and ritual gathering place commands spectacular views across to Harter Fell and Skawfell.

The great Brats Hill Stone Circle has four burial cairns within it, and each of the other four circles in this complex surrounds at least one internal burial cairn.

The warmer and more clement weather Britain experienced during the Bronze Age allowed prehistoric farmers to cultivate land that we would not consider possible today. Towards the end of the first millennium the climate deteriorated, and these farmers were forced to move off Burn Moor and down into the valley, leaving an architectural legacy behind them. To the north there is a hut circle settlement and nearby are the remains of a cairn field. Few remains have been found due to acidic soil.

Merrivale Menhir and Stone Circle
Dartmoor, Devon

Dartmoor during the Bronze Age was home to a thriving community. The climate was much less severe then than it is today. With the onset of colder and more hostile weather, these pastures were abandoned. A legacy of numerous enigmatic monuments is all that remains.

Merrivale Stone Circle (seen on the horizon) is not large, and is now much depleted – it only has eleven stones. The adjacent menhir is more than ten feet tall. Many menhirs have been used over the centuries as ancient trackway markers, and this one may well have indicated the Merrivale Stone Circle to the townsfolk of Tavistock. In 1625 the citizenry was struck down with the plague and, to avoid contamination, they and the Dartmoor community used Merrivale Stone Circle as a market place.

King Arthur's Hall
St Breward, Bodmin Moor, Cornwall

The earliest documentation of what has become known as King Arthur's Hall is from 1584, and the site has changed little in the last 400 years. This enigmatic prehistoric structure breaking the skyline is situated across King Arthur's Down, from the moorland hamlet of St Breward. Retaining the inner side of a bank, fifty-six moss-and-lichen-covered stones – some as tall as five feet – form an incomplete rectangle measuring 150 by 60 feet. There is a narrow entrance in the south-west corner, whose interior is now lower than the surrounding moor. It is damp and boggy and often under water.

The purpose of this early Celtic monument has remained a mystery. Not far away there are two Bronze Age, ruined stone circles, and hut circles and prehistoric field systems are scattered across King Arthur's Down.

Callanish Standing Stones
Callanish, Isle of Lewis, Outer Hebrides

These stones stand triumphant on a hill overlooking Loch Roag on the west coast of the Isle of Lewis. Second only in importance to Stonehenge and Avebury, Callanish can be seen for miles.

The flattened circle is only twenty-eight feet across and is made up of thirteen giant 'undressed' stones surrounding a small cist. A parallel avenue of twenty-nine stones, 250 yards long, leads up to the circle and beyond. Two other shorter 'arms' extend from the centre to the east and the west, making the shape of a Celtic cross when seen from the air.

The eminent Oxford mathematician Professor Alexander Thom, who spent a lifetime detailing stone circle alignments, believed – as many do – that these monuments could be used to calculate the precise movement of the moon from one solstice to another by aligning individual stones with points on the horizon. Numerous legends are associated with this monument. One claims that the stones represent thirteen giants who refused to be converted to Christianity and, in a most unchristian act, St Kieran turned them into stone.

Beddarthur

*Prescelly Mts, Nr Crymych,
Pembrokeshire*

Beddarthur, or Arthur's Grave, is across the valley from Carn Menyn and is usually described as an oval stone circle. This small, twelve-stone prehistoric monument, however, is more like two parallel lines of stones with one end closed. It lies upland from Carn Arthur and just below Carn Bica. Of course, King Arthur is not buried here, and more than likely he is not buried at any of the other prehistoric sites that claim to be his burial place. This is a Bronze Age temple, more than 2,500 years old. Once, these dramatic rolling hills with mysterious outcrops of rock were the home to a thriving Celtic community. The builders of this temple may well have been the same prehistoric Celts who set about transporting the mysterious bluestones to Stonehenge.

Carn Menyn

*Prescelly Mts, Nr Crymych,
Pembrokeshire*

This hillside of frost-shattered rocks is the home of the famous bluestones – so called because when wet they take on a blue hue. Eighty in all, weighing over four tons each, they were quarried from these mountains and then transported by Bronze Age man nearly 200 miles to Salisbury Plain, and Stonehenge. There is much speculation regarding just how and why these stones were transported to Salisbury Plain, to eventually become part of Stonehenge. Why these particular stones were chosen has remained a mystery and may well always remain so. Whatever the reason, it is more than probable that these prehistoric Celtic people believed that the bluestones of the Prescelly Mountains had some special significance. Were these mountains holy? Did these stones have some magical properties?

**Stonehenge, and Druids
at Stonehenge during
Summer Solstice**
Nr Amesbury, Wiltshire

This enigmatic monument,
attracting over a million visitors a
year, is situated just off the busy
A303. There have been many
theories as to who built it, what
it is, and how it got there. The
first written record of Stonehenge
was provided by Geoffrey of
Monmouth. He wrote in the
twelfth century that it was brought
by a tribe of giants from Africa,
and also that it was flown from
Ireland by the wizard Merlin. John
Aubrey, the seventeenth-century
archaeologist, claimed that it was
the Temple of the Sun, where
Druids practised ritual human
sacrifice.

We now know that, although
it was most probably used by
the Druids of ancient times as
a meeting place and a centre for
their religious cult, they only
came to Salisbury Plain 2,000
years after the first stones were
put in place. According to the
late Professor Richard Atkinson,
who excavated the site extensively and was the leading authority
on Stonehenge, it was built in
three different stages spanning
700 years, first starting around
2,200 BC.

Ysbyty Cynfyn Stone Circle
*St John the Baptist Church,
Ysbyty Cynfyn Church, Nr
Devil's Bridge, Ceredigion*

All that now remains of what was once a Bronze Age stone circle are four standing stones, and these have been incorporated into the circular wall of Ysbyty Cynfyn Church, built in the late nineteenth century. Two of these ancient stones have been moved to form a gate post, while the others are more probably in their original positions. One of them is pointed and over twelve feet tall. This ancient pagan Celtic temple, and now a place of Christian worship, shows clearly its continuity as a religious site.

Circles have been associated with death since pre-Christian times. Memorial stones in pagan times were marked with a circle, and stone circles have been used since those times as religious and ceremonial places, very often the dead being buried within them. Early Christians were encouraged in this practice by Pope Gregory in AD 601, and Patrick, Bishop of the Hebrides, who commanded Orlygus, '. . . to build a church where ever he found pagan stone circles or menhirs'.

Rollright Stone Circle
Little Rollright, Oxfordshire

In the eighteenth century the antiquarian William Stukeley wrote of the Rollright Stones as 'the greatest Antiquity we have yet seen . . . corroded like a wormeaten wood by the harsh Jaws of Time'. The Rollright Stones are one of the most celebrated stone circles in Britain. There are seventy-seven lumps of leprous limestone forming a perfect circle. Tradition has it that it is impossible to count them all. In a field across the road, and on slightly higher ground, a tall outlyer, known as the King Stone, can be found.

In the past these stones were accorded magic powers that could increase a woman's chances of conception. Traditionally barren young women would visit the circle at midnight and press the tips of their breasts against the stones, presumably in the company of their loved ones. Stukeley described groups of young people meeting at the Rollright Stones 'at a special time and make merry with cakes and ale'. Not a lot has changed – each summer, travelling theatre groups perform Shakespeare on balmy summer evenings in the prehistoric circle to local aficionados, resplendent in their finest attire.

The Adam and Eve Stones
Beckhampton Avenue
Avebury, Wiltshire

The Beckhampton Avenue, which leads westward from Avebury stone circle, is now hardly visited at all compared with the rest of the complex. The serpentine-like avenue ran along the lane that now leads past the church and into the fields, where the two longstones – Adam and Eve – can been seen, isolated against the sky. The avenue eventually ends near where the Beckhampton roundabout is now situated. By 1800 it was almost completely destroyed by men such as farmer Robinson. However, this did not happen before the Lincolnshire doctor-turned-clergyman and antiquarian William Stukeley, recorded its destruction in his charming topographical drawings. Many of the stones since those times have now been 'rediscovered'.

Avebury's more famous avenue – this being more complete – is now known as the West Kennet Avenue. It snakes its way defined by a series of distinctively shaped stones to The Sanctuary, found one and a half miles to the south.

Avebury Henge and Stone Circle
Avebury, Wiltshire

Avebury Henge and Triple Stone Circle is the largest prehistoric monument in Europe, covering twenty-eight acres and encompassing most of the village of Avebury. This huge and mysterious megalithic monument was built in around 2,000 BC, and was undoubtedly used as a ritual and ceremonial meeting place. The importance of Avebury is well illustrated by the complexity of its prehistoric architectural features and the time that it must have taken to build. Four thousand years later, it is still in places up to fifty feet in height.

The largest of the three stone circles is the outer ring, which followed the line of the ditch. This contained as many as a hundred, forty-ton stones – twenty-seven now remain. Used as a defensive position by both the invading Saxons (a Saxon army road runs through the site) and defending Britons, it is surprising that not much damage to the site was incurred until the fourteenth century. Then, in a purge on paganism by Christian zealots, many of the stones were methodically buried.

Grey Wethers
Lockridge, Wiltshire

'Wether' is the Old English name for sheep. These large lumps of rock are know as Grey Wethers because, according to folklore, in half light they resemble grey, wet, sleeping sheep. In fact, these are sarsen rocks, fragments that formed a cap on the chalk rock created millions of years ago.

At Lockridge, a picturesque hamlet near Marlborough, there are two fields under the care of the National Trust. Once, this part of the Salisbury Plain was covered with 'Grey Wethers'. Prehistoric man used them in the construction of megalithic monuments such as Avebury, Stonehenge and the Devil's Den, amongst others in Wiltshire

The Devil's Den
Nr Marlborough, Wiltshire

The Devil's Den is situated just north of the A4 between Avebury and Marlborough at Clatford Bottom.

This cromlech was probably first recorded by the antiquarian William Stukeley during the early part of the eighteenth century in his *View of the Kist-Vaen in Clatford Bottom*. He is shown, along with two companions, investigating and sketching the monument. In his time, there were three other large boulders at the base of the monument, which now appear to have been destroyed. In the distance, his coach and horses are seen along a sarsen-boulder-strewn valley bottom. In the intervening years the capstone was dislodged and the whole assembly of stones was re-erected in 1921. Although the immediate area was once covered in sarsen stones, now there are very few left. Apparently you could once walk for two miles from Delling to the main road at Clatford without stepping off them. The last order of sarsen stones from this area was in 1938. Four cart-loads were taken and used in repair work on Windsor Castle.

The Queen's Stone
Nr Goodrich, Hereford and Worcester

According to folklore this enigmatic Bronze Age monolith was known as Cwen Stan, 'Woman's Stone', but during the passage of time it has taken on a regal air. The Queen's Stone, as it is now known, stands in a loop of the River Wye, a mile west of Goodrich. The monolith is six feet tall and has eleven deep grooves – five down the south face, three on the north, one on the west and two on the east. Each groove is about eight inches deep and, when excavated, it was found that the grooves stopped at ground level.

The grooving on the monolith is most unusual. The Devil's Arrows at Boroughbridge, North Yorkshire, are similarly marked, as are some of the stones on Machrie Moor on the Isle of Arran. Nobody knows their meaning, and probably if there ever were a meaning it died with the stone's creators. However, various theories have been put forward over the years, one suggesting that sacrificial wicker baskets would have been placed above the stone and held in position with stakes placed in the grooves. Another, more humdrum explanation is that the grooves have been caused by weathering.

Kintraw Standing Stone and Cairn
Kintraw, Strathclyde

This huge megalithic-like totem pole twelve feet tall stands as a marker between two cairns, both now ruined. The larger of the cairns was originally strewn with a mass of brilliant white crystals.

The first Celts chose this place for their dead because of its magnificent view across the sparkling Loch Craignish and its many small islands; the diminutive Eilean Inshaig, Eilean Mhic Chrion, Eilean Dubh, and the larger Eilean Righ, and on to Papa Jura twenty-seven miles away. On summer days, visitors from this vantage point can be dazzled by the bright white and colourful sails of boats streaking through the deep blue water that surrounds the small picturesque holiday resort of Ardfern.

Sculptured stones, cup-and-ring-marked rocks, ancient Celtic chapels (now ruined), forts, and other monoliths dot this prehistoric Celtic landscape.

Ballymeanoch Standing Stones
Nr Kilmartin, Argyll and Bute, Strathclyde

Towards the southern end of 'The Valley of the Dead' near Kilmartin, is a group of parallel standing stones. One row is of two large stones and, to the east, is a row now comprising four giant stones. One of these stones is heavily 'cup' marked. Nobody knows the meaning of these marks, which are often accompanied by 'ring' marks. In Britain, these intriguing prehistoric symbols are most commonly found in Northumberland and Scotland. Elsewhere in Europe, these and very similar symbols have been found carved on and inside megalithic monuments, thus allowing archaeologists to date them. Along with spiral carving, they appear to be some form of prehistoric tomb art.

The six standing stones that remain are probably all that is left of a stone avenue leading up to the Nether Largie Tombs. They are adjacent to a ruinous henge monument with two burial cists. Until the end of the nineteenth century, a megalith across the field was used in a symbolic ceremony to seal wedding vows.

Templewood Stone Circle and Cist
Kilmartin, Argyll and Bute, Strathclyde

This perfect circle of thirteen stones, thirteen metres in diameter, has at its centre a small slab cist, which is surrounded by another very small ring of stones. Here the body of a child once lay, and with it a beaker and some flints. To the east, another small cist can be detected. The primary burial took place between 2,000 and 1,500 BC. There is evidence of cremation in both cists, which were then covered with a large stone cairn forming a burial mound. The most northerly stone in the circle has a spiral pattern inscribed near its base. Unfortunately this is now very faint.

Templewood Stone Circle and Cist lie to the west in the Kilmartin Valley, known dramatically as 'The Valley of the Dead', and this 'cult' site was a burial ground for thousands of years. Here, great leaders as well as their subjects were laid to rest. Adjacent to the Templewood site is another small circle and to the east is the great, linear, Bronze Age Nether Largie Barrows, as well as numerous other enigmatic megaliths.

Maen Llia, and Maen Madoc
Nr Ystradfellte, Powys

This carefully fashioned, diamond-shaped standing stone is twelve feet tall but only two feet thick. It is of Bronze Age origin, and may be a territorial marker. Diamond-shaped stones are not common, the most famous being the one that forms part of the West Kennet Avenue at Avebury, Wiltshire. Another forms part of one of the stone circles called The Hurlers at Minions in Cornwall. The significance of these stones is lost, but according to legend this one is reputed to drink from the River Nedd whenever it hears a cock crow.

Nearby a huge eleven-foot-tall monolith called Maen Madoc is inscribed in crude Latin capitals, still just legible: *Dervaci filius ivsti, ic iacti* (Dervacus, the son of Justus here he lies). It is situated at the edge of Sarn Helen, the Roman road running from Heol Senni to about two miles north of Ystradfellte. Was Dervacus a Roman? No, according to Sir Cyril Fox, who excavated Maen Madoc over fifty years ago and found no remains. Whoever erected this monument to him deliberately cut through the metalling of what was then an already overgrown Roman road.

Platform Cairn, Llyn Brenig
Nr Cerrigydrudion, Conwy

Over 3,000 years ago this lonely moor was the ritual burial ground of Bronze Age clan chiefs. There are numerous barrows of different types here, but the most interesting of all is the Platform Cairn, which is essentially a funerary monument. Situated on high ground, affording dazzling views towards Snowdon and the Cader Iris, it was made of large boulders to form a circle, whose upper surface was finished off with a flat layer of slabs. These were surrounded by a perfect circle of stones. The primary burial was of a child and adult, accompanied by a bone-handled knife and a food vessel. A large hole was left, which once held a formidable pole, perhaps something like a totem pole around which people may have danced. At a later date, the pole was removed and the hole filled in with loose stones, and the monument was covered over. Simultaneously, a small semicircular cairn was added to one side, a small hole was created and pure charcoal was placed in the hollow, which was then covered by an inverted urn.

Kerb Cairn, Llyn Brenig
Nr Cerrigydrudion, Conwy

The site also includes a Bronze Age kerb cairn – a small ring of boulders forming a stone circle filled in with loose stones. Archaeologists discovered an infant's ear bones in an urn at the centre of one cairn, implying some form of ritual sacrifice since no other bones were found. Speculation suggests that, after being offered to the gods, the children's brains were ripped out, Inca style. Could they have been eaten? The ear bones, which come from deep inside the head, were then placed in an urn and given a ritual burial.

Swinside Stone Circle
Nr Broadgate, Broughton in Furness, Cumbria

This dazzling and beautifully preserved stone circle is two miles up Swinside Farm track on private farmland. A sign advises visitors to leave their cars and walk.

Cumbrian stone circles, of which there are more than twenty recorded, are some of the largest and finest in the country. According to archaeologists, they are the earliest stone circles in Britain. Here, fragments of charcoal and burnt bones were found during excavations.

According to legend, the Devil prevented the construction of a church here. Systematically he destroyed the work done each day on church building, by causing the stones to sink into the ground each night. The site is sometimes also known as Sunkenkirk Stone Circle.

Loch Buie Stone Circle
Isle of Mull, Argyll and Bute

This small and isolated circle lies in the shadow of Ben Buie, at the far end of the road that leads to this magnificent loch. Its makers constructed their ritual monument on the only flat, arable land found along this mountainous southern coast. It has two outlyers, one small and the other considerable larger than any of the stones in the circle. The larger outlyer may well have been used as a pointer, leading prehistoric men down to the sandy beach. Significantly, it has also been shown that it can be aligned to the midwinter sunset.

Here, possibly no more than an extended family hunted, farmed and fished. Their life expectancy was not great. Evidence collected from Scottish burials of this period suggests that slightly more than fifty per cent of men lived to be older than thirty-six, while eighty-five per cent of women died before they were twenty-five – seemingly many in childbirth. A woman's first child was born by the time she reached the age of fifteen and infant death was high. Acute infection and inadequate nourishment were the main causes of death.

Longstone Cross
Minions, Cornwall

The Longstone Cross stands erect and proud on the road that leads from King Doniert's stone to Minions. Situated on the edge of the village, the monument was quite possibly once a prehistoric pagan menhir. If this was the case, this stone would have been Christianized by Celtic holy men by carving a round-headed cross on it during the Dark Ages. Its original purpose has now been lost in the mists of time.

Nearby is the spectacular Bronze Age triple stone circle known as The Hurlers, as well as other prehistoric Celtic sites.

Stowe's Pound and The Devil's Chair
Minions, Cornwall

On the often bleak summit of Stowe's Hill are two Bronze Age enclosures, collectively known as Stowe's Pound. The larger and more distinct of the two contains at least thirty-nine hut circles. There is a well-defined entrance and the tumble-wall of stone is fifteen feet high in places. However, what distinguishes Stowe's Pound from other early Celtic sites is that within its boundary are some extraordinary, weather-worn, natural granite tors. The two most famous of these are known as The Devil's Chair and The Cheesewring.

From The Devil's Chair one can see a vast landscape scattered with prehistoric Celtic sites. For example, the triple stone circles known as The Hurlers and The Rillaton Round Barrow – which contained the famous and unique Rillaton Gold Cup, lost for many years until it turned up in the dressing room of King George V.

Priddy Nine Barrows
Priddy, Somerset

This windswept Somerset farming community was once the centre of a Bronze Age community. Priddy Nine Barrows is an impressive grouping of Bronze Age barrows, many of them more than three metres high, forty-five metres in diameter. Across the field is another grouping of barrows known as Ashen Hill Barrows, and nearby is now a very distinct triple Neolithic Bronze Age henge monument. Once populous, Priddy is now best known as a centre for cavers and potholers. For one week during August a colourful group of travelling gypsies stage the annual Priddy Horse Fair. Oversized, shiny chrome trailers jostle with traditional painted caravans and benders (tarpaulin covered igloo shaped tents) for a pitch on the village green. Gypsies will tell your fortune, while muscular young men ride bareback up and down the road to show off their mounts. Others will teach the unwary
the rudiments of the Three Card Trick.

Four Round Barrows
The Ridgeway, Nr Avebury, Wiltshire

Round barrows, which are burial mounds, date principally from the Bronze Age. There are many on Marlborough Downs, and these four on Overton Hill are easily accessible where The Ridgeway is dissected by the A4, a mile east of Avebury and the West Kennet Avenue.

Round barrows come in a great variety of sizes and in four distinctly different designs. There is the 'bowl' design, which is the most common, as well as the 'bell', the 'saucer' and the 'pond'. Some round barrows can be found in isolation, others in distinctive barrows' cemeteries, while others are aligned. They tend to be sited on high ground, and would have been seen in silhouette from below.

Burial within the round barrows was by inhumation, where the deceased were laid in a crouching position and cremated along with possessions considered useful in the afterlife as well as with urns containing food offerings for the gods.

IRON AGE

Saint Michael's Mount
Marazion, Cornwall

This popular holiday destination, spectacularly set in the sweep of Mounts Bay, south of Marazion, is joined to the mainland by a causeway. Diodorus Siculus, the Greek historian writing in AD 70 called this island Ictis, and it was from here, an important port, that Cornish tin was traded with Mediterranean countries. Since pre-Norman times the Mount has been the centre of Celtic Christianity. After the Norman conquest it became subordinate to the Benedictine Abbey at Mont St Michel in Brittany. During the medieval period, the Celtic community grew and the island became one of the most important pilgrimage centres in Cornwall. Since 1659, the Mount has been the home of the St Aubyn family, who still retain private apartments there. Lord and Lady St Levan gave the island to the National Trust in 1954, and during the season both it and the grounds are open to the public. Legend claims that two fisherman saw a vision of St Michael, hence the island's name, while another states that St Michael visited a hermit living on the island.

The Iron Age marks the beginning of a cycle of development when iron came into common usage, replacing bronze as a standard material for implements and weapons. This is the final phase of the three sequences in prehistoric Britain, known as the Stone, Bronze and Iron Ages. In Britain, this period lasted nearly 700 years, and it was one of continual change.

The landscape of Iron Age Britain is characterized by the profusion of hillforts that dot the countryside. Traditionally it is thought that these were times of considerable trouble, intertribal conflict and invasion. The hillforts of Britain varied enormously in size: some were extremely large and were, in fact, the first towns; while others were small and used only by extended families for their own protection. One of these first towns was at Traprain Law in South Lothian, which had as many as 2 to 3,000 people living there at any one time. By the first century BC some of these 'towns' were organized. There is evidence to indicate that housing was built over many years, with old houses being demolished and new ones constructed on their foundations. Some 'streets' were built in straight rows, with rubbish pits dug behind the housing. Some 'towns' adopted zoning systems: craftsmen worked in one area, food was stored in another, while animals were kept in a third. The British Camp, though smaller than Traprain Law, was extremely heavily fortified, with double and triple ramparts and ditches. The construction of these fortifications would have been a formidable task involving probably the whole community. The bedrock may have been broken with wooden wedges by the men, then the children might have cleared the waste material away using wooden shovels, filling baskets that the women carried away and emptied in piles to form the ramparts. Other hillforts were much smaller and were little more than fortified positions used by particular family groups – Torr a' Chaisteal Dun on the Isle of Arran is an example of this type. Small settlements, such as Carn Euny in Cornwall and at Jarlshof in Shetland, developed due to the particular circumstances of the local population. There are also countless examples of single dwellings called round houses. The round houses below Holyhead Mountain Hillfort on Anglesey were occupied well before the Iron Age. These originally consisted of more than fifty buildings covering between fifteen and twenty acres. Radiocarbon dating techniques indicate that the site was in use from the late Neolithic period until the Dark Ages, some 5 or 6,000 years. There are eighteen distinct dwellings or farm buildings. However, no more than two were in use at any one time. The occupiers were farmers, who supplemented their diet by eating a variety of shellfish, principally limpets. The tradition of living beneath the Holyhead Hillfort continues to this day. The dwellings that now abut this archaeological site, however, are small white bungalows neatly trimmed in black, wooden-lattice frames.

Though these were troubled times, it would be wrong to assume that Britain was continually at war. Ninety-nine per cent of the population were occupied in food production. Britain was a nation of small farmers; thickly wooded landscapes were separated by a patchwork of small fields that could typically be ploughed in a day. These were divided by hedges and bounded by stone banks. Corn and barley were grown, numerous pigs, sheep and cattle were kept. Oxen were used to pull the new iron ploughs and small horses were also bred. These Iron Age people also bred certain animals that were revered. Julius Caesar notes that the cockerel, the hare and the goose were never eaten. Queen Boudicca of the Iceni is supposed to have released a hare while invoking Andraste, a goddess of battle and victory, before setting out on her bloody and short-lived victorious campaign against the Romans. Dogs were kept as pets and as working animals – indeed, much as hill farmers would today. Some Celtic field patterns are still visible, and in Cornwall the farmers in the remote and isolated hamlet of Treen still farm many of the same field systems. Little has changed in 2,000 years. Festivals broke the pattern of farming, particularly Samain, a fertility festival at the end of the year when the ritual slaughter of the animals that would not be kept through the winter months took place. Samain was celebrated towards the end of October and the beginning of November – our modern Hallowe'en celebrations are a pale reflection of this great Celtic occasion.

Their society was a complex one, but it is only in its last one hundred years or so that it may well have been based on a hierarchical principle, with a clan chief or king ruling over his followers. In Ireland, this was called a tuath. Each king had a derbfine – a group of several generations, or an extended family. On his death, any member of the derbfine could succeed him and inherit, since there was no line of succession. All land was held in common ownership. Below this level of society were the nobles and the warrior class, who counted their wealth by the amount of cattle that they possessed. Julius Caesar, when confronted with Iron Age Celts, marvelled at these warriors and, in particular, at their use of chariots in battle. He explained how before battle commenced these painted and ferocious warriors drove all about the battlefield hurling spears and javelins. The noise and the speed of the horses often caused the enemy to break rank. Then after making their way through their own ranks, they dismounted and proceeded on foot, their charioteers returning and placing the chariots conveniently in case their masters needed a quick means of retreat. Caesar concluded that these warriors combined the mobility of cavalry and the staying power of foot soldiers.

The farmers, who paid a food rent to the clan chief, followed the warrior class, and at the bottom of the social pyramid were the slaves. Quite apart from these groups were the Aes Dana class, who were the craftsmen, musicians, lawyers and doctors, and these learned men included among their number the religious leaders whom Julius Caesar called the Druids. Iron age Celts produced in their workshops fine treasures in amber, gold, silver and other precious metals, for the élite of society, and their designs were extraordinarily stylish. Heavy, twisted, gold neck collars and torcs, which were worn by both men and women, as well as armlets and bracelets have been found. The wealthiest wore dyed garments interwoven with gold – which, according to contemporary writers, looked as if they were 'sprinkled with gold' – and these were fastened with cleverly jewelled clasps. They also carried swords, spears and daggers that had been beautifully decorated with intricately patterned metalwork.

Trade took place with European and Mediterranean countries. The Greeks, for example, are known to have sought tin. Diodorus Siculus wrote that the natives of this part of Britain (southern Cornwall) were friendly to strangers who came to trade. They produced the tin carefully into ingots shaped like knuckle bones, which were traded from an island called Ictis, which we now suppose referred to St Michael's Mount.

Garn Fawr Iron Age Hillfort
Strumble Head, Pembrokeshire

This Iron Age hillfort is one of the finest in Wales. On a fair day it is possible to see the Wicklow Hills in Ireland, and Snowdon and the Lleyn Peninsula in north Wales. To the south is the wild, rugged scenery of Dinas Mawr and the promontory Iron Age hillfort. Beyond, Abercastle and Careg Samson, and beyond still further is St David's Head, the home of Celtic tribesmen for many centuries.

Its commanding position, 700 feet up a steep rockface, has been put to good use many times since this Celtic Iron Age hillfort was first established. To the north-west are the arable farms of Strumble Head and Caregwastad Point – the scene of the last invasion of Britain. In 1797 French troops, led by an American called Tate, surrendered as they were unable to land at Bristol. According to legend, they mistook the red-caped local women for red-coated British troops

Over a hundred years later, during the First World War, this site was once again used as a lookout position and a compass was carved in the rockface.

Careg Samson
Nr Abercastle, Pembrokeshire

This magnificent Neolithic cromlech is perhaps at least 5,000 years old and takes its name from a local Celtic Christian, St Samson. Now largely forgotten, he was born in Dyfed of noble parentage and after being educated at Llanwit Major eventually became the Abbot of Caldey Island, as well as of Dol in Brittany. He later became the Archbishop of York. In this part of west Wales there are numerous prehistoric sites as well as natural ones that bear his name.

The mighty leader whose last resting place this is, looks out across a meadow, and up this wild windswept coast, past an islet at Abercastle where the Grave of Samson's finger can be found. Further on, one can see Garn Fawr and Dinas Mawr on Strumble Head (seen in the distance with cloud cover), where the remains of a Celtic Iron Age fort dating to approximately 100 BC can be found.

The British Camp
Little Malvern, Hereford and Worcester

This huge Iron Age hillfort is one of two adjacent hillforts – The British Camp and Midsummer Hill Camp – which are known collectively as the Hereford Beacon Forts. The huge contour-hugging ramparts of The British Camp enclose a site of thirteen hectares. There has been no systematic excavation of the original Iron Age fort, but evidence suggests that The British Camp was a permanent village for some considerable time, with a population of about 2,000. They lived in small wood-and-daub houses that had been methodically laid out over the whole area, and kept their cattle in the pastures below the fort, where some Celts may well have lived. Surprisingly there is no permanent water supply within the fort, and interestingly for such a large and permanently occupied village, no Iron Age cemetery has ever been found either. The British Camp is unusual in that during the twelfth century a Norman 'citadel' was constructed at the summit, within the original Iron Age fort. Nothing now remains of what is thought to have been a small wooden castle.

The Wrekin
Nr Telford, Shropshire

This impressive hillfort, with a commanding view towards Wales across the flat arable land of Shropshire, was probably first used during the Bronze Age period. At the south-west end there are the remains of a barrow. Later it was used by Iron Age people, and then again during the Roman occupation of Britain, when it was possibly the tribal capital of the Cornovii, who were then settled four miles away at Viroconium Cornoviorum by the Romans.

The fort takes up much of the hill, about ten hectares. An inner defensive position was built first, followed by surrounding earth banks. To add to its impregnability, these Celts then set about scraping away the hill to create an artificially steep incline. There is evidence of permanent occupation on the site – post holes and the remains of hut flooring have been found, along with evidence of storage pits and guttering.

The Wrekin is one of the few hillforts that, with little change, still retains its original name: Oriconion.

Carn Euny Fogou
Nr Penzance, Cornwall

The prehistoric village settlement at Carn Euny is over 2,000 years old. There is evidence of earlier occupation, but the site is primarily Iron Age. The people who lived here were farmers, who continually adapted their housing over many hundreds of years. The Carn Euny Fogou was first discovered by miners during the nineteenth century. It is an underground chamber that was probably built during the latter part of the Iron Age and its name comes from the Cornish word for cave.

It was built in three successive stages, and was originally closed at each end. Entrance was via a very small 'creep' passage. Various theories exist as to the function of a fogou. They could have been used for hiding in during times of trouble, or for storage. However, scholars believe that they may have served some religious purpose. In the Carn Euny Fogou, a unique and distinctive type of pottery was found and this is now known as Carn Euny Ware.

Jarlshof Bronze Age House
Sumburgh, Shetland

The Jarlshof Bronze Age settlement is one of the most complete, and is perhaps one of the longest continually occupied sites in the British Isles. The settlement, on the southern tip of Shetland, was in use from the late Neolithic period throughout the Bronze and Iron Ages and also during the period of Viking occupation, and then intermittently to the sixteenth century.

A British Pompeii, on the edge of the sea, over hundreds of years successive waves of sand have engulfed this settlement. However, that never stopped other settlers setting up, and rebuilding and adapting existing houses. During the Bronze Age, a smith built a workshop, for example, in a dilapidated Neolithic building. During the Pictish period several small sunken-floored turf houses were built, and these are associated on this site with two souterrains. The site was lost below a protective blanket of sand until a storm in 1897 re-exposed part of the settlement.

Lomond Hill
Nr Kinross, Perth and Kinross

South of Dundee on the A91, the Lomond Hills form part of a spectacular ridge that includes the Iron Age hillforts of Maiden Castle and East Lomond Hillfort. West Lomond Hill has on its summit the remains of an enormous prehistoric cairn that is now ten feet high and measures eighty-eight by ninety-six feet. It is in ruinous condition, having been vandalized over the thousands of years since it was built, presumably for some great clan chief. It has not been excavated since the beginning of the nineteenth century, when it was noted as being considerably larger than it is now. Human bones buried to a depth of seven feet were found, along with the remains of a cinerary urn.

To the south-west is Loch Leven, now a National Nature Reserve. The largest island in this loch is named after St Serf who rescued, brought up, and baptized Kentigern before sending him on his way to Glasgow.

Traprain Law Iron Age Hillfort
Nr Haddington, East Lothian

During the Iron Age, Traprain Law was the capital of a tribe called the Votadini, who occupied south-east Scotland. They were a rich and powerful tribe working fertile land from which they derived much of their wealth. As many as 2,000 people lived here. During the Roman advances in the latter part of the first century AD, they allied themselves with these invaders. Traprain Law remained their capital after the departure of the Romans up until the end of the fifth century, when they lost power to the invading Angles, by which time their 'city' had moved to Edinburgh.

According to folklore, King Loth, who ruled and gave his name to the region, had a daughter called Thenaw. She fell in love and became pregnant, but the match was unsuitable. Her father decreed that she must die. She and her son, Kentigern, miraculously survived. He was brought up by the aged St Serf who had rescued them and nicknamed him Mungo. Eventually Mungo moved to Glasgow where he founded a religious community, and later became the city's patron saint. His mother followed and was canonized as St Enoch.

Tre'r Ceiri Hillfort
Llanaelhaearn, Gwynedd

Tre'r Ceiri is possibly the best example of an Iron Age hillfort in southern Britain, and is certainly the most complete in Wales. It is situated 1,800 feet up on the most easterly of the three peaks that make up Yr Eifl Mountain. Tre'r Ceiri, 'The Town of Giants', commands panoramic views over the whole area. Built during the centuries prior to the Roman occupation of Wales in AD 78, and occupied until the fourth century, the five-acre site consists of a huge perimeter wall that encircles about 130 hut circles. Some hut circles are square, others oblong, and some circular living spaces have been divided to form two dwellings.

Few artefacts have ever been found, and no burials seem to have been carried out here. However, a Bronze Age cairn looks down on 'The Town of Giants' from the very summit.

Howling winds, and a steep climb to and from the pasture land below meant that these Celtic farmers, besides having someone to fear, must have been extremely hardy people.

Old Oswestry Hillfort
Oswestry, Shropshire

This magnificent fortress is one mile north of Oswestry. It encloses just over fifteen acres and has an elaborate defensive system of ramparts. Excavation shows that Neolithic people first occupied this dominating position during the fifth and sixth centuries BC, but the site was then abandoned. From the Iron Age through to the Roman period, it was continually occupied.

Within the traversing ramparts are two unique, huge, deep and mysterious annexes, which were once thought to be able to hold water. Other researchers have speculated that they may have been used to corral cattle. Both of these suggestions have now, however, been rejected.

This fort was once known as Caer Ogyrfan, the fort of Gogrvan, who was the father of Guinevere, wife of King Arthur – a romantic notion but pure folktale.

Ty Mawr Hut Circle and Holyhead Mountain
Holyhead, Anglesey

The Ty Mawr Hut Circle Group, also known as the Cytian Gwyddelod, 'The Irishmen's Huts', originally consisted of over fifty buildings covering between fifteen and twenty acres. Radio-carbon dating the artefacts excavated indicate that the site was in use from the late Neolithic period until the Dark Ages – some 5 or 6,000 years. There are eighteen distinct dwellings or farm buildings, however, but no more than two were in use at any one time. The occupiers were farmers who supplemented their diet by eating a variety of shellfish.

The hut circle group lies at the foot of Holyhead Mountain and the Iron Age hillfort of Caer y Twr. Seventeen acres are enclosed by a now very ruinous stone wall. These sites are adjacent to the South Stacks Cliff Nature Reserve, where numerous sea birds, including coughs, guillemots, razorbills, kittiwakes and puffins, linnets, stonechats, wrens, and white-throats, as well as more than twenty-five species of butterfly, can be found.

Dinas Bran
Llangollen, Denbighshire

Dinas Bran is dominated by the ruin of a medieval castle, which commands the Vale of Llangollen. About 1,000 feet above sea-level, this surprisingly conical and naturally shaped hill was held during the eighth century by Eliseg, the Prince of Powys.

Built on the site of an Iron Age hillfort, the ramparts are still visible. This site was once occupied by Bran the Blessed, who, in Welsh legend, was originally a god demoted after the advent of Christianity. He lived here during the Dark Ages, and this may well be the site of Bran's stronghold from the tales in the *Mabinogion*. If so, then this is the mysterious place, 'Castle of the Grail', from the Arthurian legends. Accordingly if this is the case, the Holy Grail – the cup that Christ used at the Last Supper – may well lie hidden here.

Another treasure awaits discovery; Merlin is supposed to have left a golden harp to be found by a blue-eyed boy with yellow hair accompanied by a dog with a silver eye.

Llangollen, named after the Celtic saint, Collen, is now famous for the National Eisteddfod, which has been held here each July since 1947.

Brent Knoll
Nr Weston-Super-Mare, North Somerset

This isolated hill, surrounded by the Somerset Levels and bordered by the Bristol Channel to the west and the A5 motorway to the east, is the site of an Iron Age hillfort. The fort is roughly triangular, with a single rampart and ditch. On both the west and south faces the hillside has been artificially scraped to increase the gradient and defensive position. Probably the site of many skirmishes, it was in use throughout the Roman occupation of Britain, and right up to the end of the fourth century.

According to folktale, Brent Knoll was the site of a battle between Yder, a Knight of King Arthur's Round Table, and three local giants. Yder was sent ahead to prepare the way for Arthur and his army. However, when they arrived at Brent Knoll, Arthur found that Yder and the giants were all dead.

The actual hillfort has been much denuded over the years through quarrying for lias limestone and, in more recent times, the ramparts have been used as military trenches.

St Michael's Church, an exquisite example of Norman architecture, nestles at the foot of Brent Knoll.

Chun Castle
Morvah, Cornwall

High on Penwith Moor with spectacular views, the impressive remains of Chun Castle are still apparent. Originally over 250 feet in diameter with walls eighteen feet high, this hillfort is entirely built of stone and would have once dominated this wild and windy position.

Occupied from the third century BC through to the Dark Ages, this Iron Age hillfort has been much modified. It now encloses a stone-clad well and several courtyard houses. The double entrance was cleverly realigned during the Dark Ages to provide a staggered entrance, exposing an intruder's unshielded side to the defenders. Just who those intruders might have been is open to speculation, perhaps marauding Irish pirates.

In the eighteenth century Chun Castle is recorded to have walls that were fifteen feet high. Then, during the nineteenth century when much of Penzance was built, this site was plundered for building material. Madron Workhouse, for example, was built from these stones.

Carn Brae
Redruth, Cornwall

Carn Brae lies above the former mining town of Redruth, once famous for its forest of smoking chimneys sprouting from the engine houses that provided the power for the mining shafts.

The Carn Brae prehistoric site encompasses forty-six acres. From about 3,900 BC huge stone ramparts enclosed a village occupied by over 200 people, who were peacefully settled until their community was attacked and burnt down. Archaeologists have found more than 700 arrow heads. In 1749 two hoards of Celtic coins from south-east Britain and Gaul dating from the late Iron Age were excavated.

Carn Brae Castle's origins are medieval. It was first recorded in the fifteenth century, and was probably built by the Basset family and used as a chapel and, later, a hunting lodge. It has been enlarged over the years and is now a restaurant, the granite boulder being an integral part of the building.

According to folktale, a giant named Bolster lived and fought an endless battle with another giant on Carn Brae. His strength was such that he could hurl the enormous granite boulders about, and his stride was so great that it took him just one step from St Agnes Beacon to Carn Brae.

Willapark
Boscastle, Cornwall

Willapark and its natural defensive position was typical of numerous Iron Age promontory forts built by Celtic tribesmen. A huge single bank and ditch were dug across a narrow isthmus, which gave them a secure cliff castle. Now surmounted by a white-washed look-out tower, depicted by Turner in 1827, it has variously been described as a 'pleasure house' and a 'prospect house', and in old maps and guide books it is shown as an observatory.

To the east of Willapark on Forrabury Common there are the so-called Forrabury Stitches: forty-two strips of individual land, divided only by low banks that early Celtic farmers cultivated separately. Tenants individually cultivated their strips, from Lady Day (25 March) to Michaelmas (29 September). Thereafter the land went into common usage until the following Lady Day. This land is now managed and owned by the National Trust, and during the spring and summer it is ablaze with wild flowers.

St Michael de la Rupe Church
Brentor, Devon

The church of St Michael de la Rupe is situated on the very western edge of Dartmoor and adjacent to an Iron Age fort, on an eroded cone of volcanic lava. This tor, 1,000 feet above sea level, commands spectacular views across the broad and arable plains, south to Tavistock and west to Launceston. Brentor comes from the Celtic word 'Bryn', meaning hill or mount.

St Michael de La Rupe, St Michael of the Rock, is one of the smallest churches in the country and was built by Robert Giffard, the Lord of the Manor of Lamberton and Whitechurch in about 1130. As with many ancient Norman churches it has seen numerous additions and alterations since its humble beginnings. Despite the rugged climb over often slippery and steep, grassy banks, services are still held in this wind- and rain-battered church each Sunday at 6.30pm from Easter until September.

Legend has it that the devil moved this tiny church to the top of the tor from safer ground below. St Michael, on completion of the building, beat off this evil spirit, hurling rock after rock down upon him.

Gurnards Head Cliff Castle
Treen, Cornwall

Gurnards Head Cliff Castle is protected by the usually frantic Atlantic Ocean and a sheer cliff wall. For an invading force to berth a boat and then scale the sea wall would have been an almost impossible task. On the landward side at the narrowest point of this headland, Iron Age Celtic people built three, now ruined, stone ramparts, sixty metres long, and accompanying ditches. These ramparts are slightly out of alignment and form a staggered entrance. During excavations in the 1930s, it was discovered that the inner ramparts had been built to provide steps, possibly for defensive sling shot use, similar to some Breton sites.

On the sheltered east side, more than ten Iron Age house platforms have been identified, and these were re-occupied during the Romano-British period. Gurnards Head Cliff Castle is approached by a track leading from the diminutive farming settlement of Treen, which also has associations with early Celtic, Romano-British and prehistoric settlement sites. In some cases, these can be found among the original Iron Age Celtic field pattern systems. Very little has changed here over 2,000 years.

Kenidjack Castle
St Just, Cornwall

A high, natural central spine of the rock and a triple rampart, makes this Iron Age hillfort an almost impregnable stronghold. An ancient trackway used for transporting tin and copper leads to the cliff castle from the cove below, which was once rich in minerals.

Julius Caesar wrote complaining about the difficulty in defeating these Celts, who took up a defensive position from within their cliff castles. He complained that attack from the seaward side was hazardous – at low tide it was impossible and at high tide, due to the steepness and the clever defensive network, attack was also difficult. When the defenders felt an onslaught from the landward side was imminent and impossible to beat off, they would gather their possessions and embark into one of their massive oak boats, moving off to another cliff castle further along the coast.

Drumadoon
Nr Blackwaterfoot, Isle of Arran, North Ayrshire

Drumadoon, the name means 'hill of the fort' is the largest Iron Age hillfort on Arran. Spectacularly situated, the massive enclosure of nearly twelve acres looks across Drumadoon Bay to Blackwaterfoot, with Kintyre to the west.

The natural sea cliffs offered protection from invaders, while to the landward side a very ruinous single stone wall provided protection and shelter. A single Bronze Age menhir still stands, though surprisingly for such a large fort very few hut circles have been found.

Torr a' Chaisteal Dun
Nr Corriecravie, Isle of Arran, North Ayrshire

This natural knoll may well have first been fortified 1,800 years ago. The square top contains a three-metre-thick circular stone wall of a ruined dun. Here, an extended family once lived and were undoubtedly both farmers and fishermen. These duns are often only slightly larger than a hut circle, and share many of the same architectural features of the much larger defensive forts known in northern Scotland as brochs. Torr a' Chaisteal looks out over Kilbrannan Sound, named after the sixth century Celtic saint, Brendan. When excavated during the nineteenth century it revealed little – some human bones, a grinding stone and some haematite iron.

Many duns were re-occupied through the centuries, certainly up to the Dark Ages, and it is quite likely that this one was too. If so, it may well have been used by Gaelic-speaking Irish folk called Scotti, who invaded and established themselves in Argyle 1,500 years ago.

Crannogs, Loch Awe and Loch Nell
Nr Ford and Nr Kilmore, Argyll and Bute

These small, circular islands, now a hundred yards into both Loch Awe and Loch Nell, were once the homes of lake-dwelling families. There are known to be about 400 crannogs in Scotland, but since Scotland has more than 30,000 lochs there is every chance that more will be discovered. There have been no discoveries of crannogs in England and only one in Wales.

They are essentially single family lake dwellings that were popular from the early part of the Iron Age until after the Roman occupation. However, there is now new evidence that some crannogs were first occupied as early as the Neolithic period, while others are known to have been in use up until the seventeenth century.

The foundations were built by adding boulders to a natural

rocky outcrop in a lake, which were then filled in with loose stones. From that base a wooden stilt house was constructed, probably with a reed thatch, as a sort of water-borne round house. Crannogs were attached to the land by a jetty. They were a popular form of dwelling, primarily because they afforded security from attack by both man and beast. Additionally, they were relatively pest-free and afforded an excellent fishing platform. According to recent archaeological evidence, crannog dwellers from the late Bronze-Age and early Iron Age kept cattle, sheep, goats and pigs. They were farmers who built near fertile land.

THE AGE OF THE SAINTS AND KING ARTHUR

Merlin's Cave
Tintagel, Cornwall

Merlin's Cave lies immediately below Arthur's Castle. Geoffrey of Monmouth first mentions Arthur in 1139 in his book *Historia Regum Britanniae*. In post-Roman, Celtic British legend, Arthur figures are roving war leaders, but never kings. Geoffrey of Monmouth, writing 500 years later, developed the romantic idea of King Arthur being heir to King Uther Pendragon, who, with Merlin's help, was transformed into the guise of Gorlois, Duke of Cornwall. Pendragon then made his way into Gorlois's castle and seduced his wife, Igerna. She subsequently gave birth to Arthur, who was found by Merlin. This theme was taken up in the nineteenth century by Alfred Lord Tennyson, who popularized the story in *Idylls of the King*:

But the tempest, when the long wave broke
All down the thundering shores of Bude and Bos,
There came a day as still as heaven, and then
They found a naked child upon the sands
Of dark Tintagil by Cornish sea;
And that was Arthur; and they foster'd him
Till he by miracle was approven King. . .

The Christianization of Britain by holy men and their followers has left an incredible visual legacy: the intricate and beautifully carved crosses; the extraordinary and mysterious, and still not understood Pictish cross slab carvings; the ancient holy wells; as well as the visual heritage of King Arthur, who historically is credited with uniting the Celts in their Christian struggle against the invading Angles and Saxons. This period in British history is known as the Dark Ages, a period in Britain which starts with the withdrawal of the Roman armies from Britain in AD 476 to the beginning of the tenth century. A period of re-evaluation and transition, and not as is suggested by the old name Dark Ages as one of artistic and economic decline. As the Romans gradually departed, the organizational structures that had been forced on Britain disintegrated. Long-forgotten princes and kings fought to take control of Britain, some men straddled the end of the Roman period and were able to embrace the new structure, and became the first kings of the new Britain. One such man may have been Coel Hen, otherwise known as Old King Cole of nursery rhyme fame. In what we now call Scotland and Wales, tribal kings were struggling to achieve overall supremacy and, at the same time, secure their territory from invasion by both the Vikings and marauding bands of Irish (the Scots) and Angles from the northwest. Britain was at war with itself, as well as having to contend with the invading armies of Angles, Saxons and Jutes who settled in what became Angle-land, England, during the fifth and sixth centuries.

Cars skid to a halt, some reverse noisily into the layby, doors open and slam as holiday-making families pile out. Scandinavians, Dutch, Germans, Poles and occasionally English walk past King Doniert's Stone, set in place to commemorate King Durngarth, one of the last kings of Cornwall. They stride to the English Heritage information sign, read it and then incredulously take their obligatory snap, before resuming their journey to Minions, past the Longstone Cross that stands erect and proud as a marker announcing your arrival there. This enormous and well-preserved Celtic cross has stood here since the first Christians arrived, its origin and true purpose lost, forgotten in the mist of Bodmin Moor. Times have changed. Minions in prehistory was undoubtedly a great Bronze Age gathering place. The Hurlers is testimony to that. These primitive Celts built one of the most beautiful and enigmatic stone monuments in Britain, they farmed extensively on the moor and buried their dead in great round barrows. They lived within the shadow of the Devil's Chair at Stowe's Pound. They were replaced by Iron Age Celts, whose leaders were the Druids. In time and with the advent of Christianity, the Roman Church superseded the simpler and more basic Celtic faith. That, too, was to falter and its power diminish. The industrial revolution brought once again great prosperity to this wild and windy moor. Tin-mining, which the Iron Age Celts had developed so successfully 2,000 years previously, and now quarrying made Minions a bustling village. The proprietor of a local tea room, The Hurlers Halt, told me: '. . . a hundred years ago it was possible to buy anything from a tin bath to a tin tack, and The Hurlers Halt had according to the vicar been a bordello.' Nowadays, though a tourist centre, Minions does not even boast a shop.

The holy men who set up the Longstone Cross on Bodmin Moor, probably by carving a simple round-headed cross out of an ancient pagan menhir, are now no more. However, the first Christian holy men from Ireland, Wales and Brittany who arrived in Cornwall and south-west Britain during the fourth and fifth centuries AD on evangelizing missions are not forgotten. Though none of them today has the widespread popularity that St David has in Wales, or St Columba in Scotland, nevertheless they have left their mark. There are hundreds of villages throughout Cornwall that bear the names of these saints.

After the Synod of Whitby in AD 664, Celtic Christianity was still practised, even though the Roman version was supposed to have superseded it. The first evangelizers who sailed to these shores came in small groups. They set up individual cells and baptisteries, usually in wooded valleys and always near water, which was literally life-giving. Small groups of holy men and women came together for communal meals and prayer, some lived as hermits, while others lived in family communities. Their first task was to befriend and then convert the local chiefs whose land they had settled on. As the word of the gospels they preached and their fame spread, their following grew. They formed larger communities of monks and, with their families, they lived in what is called a lan. This may have comprised several small houses, a farm and a small chapel, encompassed by a wall, which hundreds of years later became the churchyard wall, the church being built over the original chapel. There are numerous examples where this is the case. In Wales, for example, it is only a short walk along a timeworn track that leads from St Cybi's Well to the ancient church of Llangybi. In Cornwall at Sancreed Church, which is dedicated to one of two early Celtic saints, St Credan, the configuration of the churchyard suggest that this was a very early Celtic monastic site. Celtic crosses in the churchyard and others in the vicinity confirm this, as does the proximity of the ancient Sancreed 'Holy Well', which until medieval times was in common usage. There are steep, narrow steps going down into the well, which would have been used for baptism ceremonies. Even today, this place is occasionally used by local pagan groups. Votive offerings hang from the branches of nearby bushes.

These saints often travelled widely. St Samson of Dol, for example, was educated by St Illtud, who himself may originally have travelled from Brittany to set up his monastery at Llanwit Major, which in its time was one of the great centres of learning in Britain. St Samson is remembered in west Wales, where a huge cromlech is named after him along with various coastal features. He was also an abbot on Caldey Island, and is remembered in Cornwall, as well as most famously in Brittany where the great cathedral is dedicated to him. Numerous myths and legends surround many of these saints. St Ia, the patron saint of St Ives, for example, is reputed to have sailed to Cornwall on a leaf, while others came on millstones! St Beuno, a sixth-century Welsh holy man, is reputed to have restored to life not only St Winefride by placing her head back on her shoulders after it had been cut off, but also to have performed this miracle on at least one other occasion. He is best remembered in north Wales, where several churches are dedicated to him. However, St Beuno is also commemorated in Somerset at Culbone Church, which is set deep into the hillside, a good hour's walk up a steep path through an ancient forest of wind-beaten, stunted oak trees.

St Columba was born in Ireland in AD 521, and according to legend carried with him the original Stone of Destiny when he travelled to Iona in AD 563 to set up his monastery, which eventually became a great religious centre. He was aware that he needed to secure Iona's future in a land that was Pictish, pagan and hostile. He and his disciples set about converting the Picts. King Bridei was one of the first Pictish kings to have shown an interest in Christianity. Columba died in AD 597, the year that St Augustine and his missionary monks came to Britain from Rome.

Arthur, 'the once and future king' as the now famous phrase coined by Sir Thomas Malory goes, was born at the end of the fifth century, probably of Roman-British parentage. According to legend, he was born at Tintagel Castle, and though medieval, fifth- and sixth-century occupation of the island has been established, an early monastery is suspected. Evidence of great wealth and trade with Mediterranean countries dating from this time has been found, undoubtedly pointing to Tintagel being the seat of local clan chiefs and kings.

Historically Arthur is credited with uniting the Celts, by this time living mainly in the south and west of England, in their Christian struggle against the invading Saxon armies. Arthur, the leader of the Celts, was first mentioned by Nennius, a ninth-century Welsh monk, in his *Annals Cambriae*. Nennius wrote of the twelve battles that Arthur fought, and of his eventual death at the battle of Camlann with Mordred in AD 538. The ecclesiastic twelfth-century writer, Geoffrey of Monmouth, included Arthur in his book *History of the Kings of Britain*, a work based on early poems, stories and also on Breton folklore. It was Geoffrey who had Arthur being conceived at Tintagel, as the son of Uther Pendragon and Igerna, and who as a young man succeeded his father to fight a campaign against the invading Saxon armies. This heroic leader was victorious at the battle of Mount Badon, where he killed 960 men in a single day, 'no one overthrew them except himself alone'. He gave Celtic Britain forty years of peace before being mortally wounded at the battle of Camlann, to die, but yet not, and to be carried away to Avalon. Years later in popular imagination, Arthur was still alive, hiding with his Knights of the Round Table, waiting for an opportunity to return to free the Celts from their oppressors.

During his reign from 1154 to 1189, Henry II spent only twelve of those years in England – the rest of his time was spent supporting his kingdom in France. Henry visited Glastonbury soon after a devastating fire there in 1184. Much of the Abbey was destroyed, which, as an institution, had enjoyed massive patronage and endowments since it was believed that the very first Christian shrine in Britain had been built there. Disastrously the 'Old Wattle Church', which housed the Abbey's most treasured and precious possessions as well as numerous irreplaceable relics, was destroyed. Henry gave substantial sums towards its rebuilding, however pilgrims were essential to maintain the financial position and importance of the Abbey.

Shortly after Henry's death Arthur's grave was conveniently discovered by the monks. A stone cross and Latin inscription read: *Here lies entombed the renowned King Arthur with Guinevere his second wife in the Isle of Avalon.* Below it, a hollow tree trunk contained a skeleton of an unusually large man, whose skull had been deeply scarred, and also the bones of a woman, along with a lock of golden hair. Gerald of Wales writing in the twelfth century believed the monks had been put up to this. True or not, word soon spread and once more Glastonbury became a centre of pilgrimage. In 1278 these relics were reburied in front of the high altar, which was sacked during the Reformation and subsequently lost. At this time, the British and French royal courts had been joined, and it was the French writer, Chrétien de Troyes, who set King Arthur's court at Camelot and called his queen, Guinevere. This new story of Arthur, Guinevere and Sir Lancelot was printed in France. Other versions appeared in Italian, German and Spanish. The search for the Holy Grail, which originally had been a sacred vessel in pre-Christian Celtic mythology, had now become the cup that Christ had used at the Last Supper, popularly believed to have been brought to Britain by Joseph of Arimathea. Excalibur, Arthur's sword, was then found at Glastonbury, even though according to Cornish legend it had been thrown into Dozmary Pool on Bodmin Moor not far from 'Camlann'. In 1469 Thomas Malory wrote the

Arthurian cycle, which was then edited by William Caxton and printed in 1485 as *Morte D' Arthur*. By now Arthur, historically a Celtic Dark Ages leader, had been transformed into a romantic medieval king, with a band of loyal and chivalrous knights. Adding fuel to the legend, in 1542, the Tudor antiquarian John Leyland wrote what he had heard when visiting South Cadbury: 'At the very south ende of chirch of South-Cadbyri standith Camallate, sumtyme a famose toun or castelle . . . the people can telle nothing ther but that they have heard say that Arture much resortid to Camalat.'

In the nineteenth century, when Alfred Lord Tennyson, the then Poet Laureate, dedicated his *Idylls of the King* to Queen Victoria, public interest was huge and the Arthurian legends and myths had been completely re-established. Tintagel, Glastonbury and the prehistoric hillfort at South Cadbury, which historically may well have been Arthur's fort, have become the places of Arthurian legend and pilgrimage.

Today Glastonbury is the centre of Arthurian legend and of a 'New Age' culture. The picturesque town is crowded with alternative shops and health food restaurants. Besides the Abbey, the Tor with the ruins of St Michael's Church pointing like a finger upwards towards heaven, there is Wearyall Hill. The original Glastonbury Thorn once stood here, and is said, according to legend, to have sprung from the staff carried by St Joseph of Arimathea when he sailed to Britain with the Christ Child.

King Doniert's Stone
St Cleer, Cornwall

On the fringe of Bodmin Moor, on the road that runs from Redgate to Minions, are two finely engraved, ninth-century granite crosses, now without cross heads. The taller of the two is decorated with an interlacing carving, while the shorter granite slab is patterned as well as inscribed: *Doniert Progavit Anima*, (Doniert ordered [this cross] for [the good of] his soul).

Doniert is often thought to have been King Durngarth, who is incorrectly believed to have been the last King of Cornwall and drowned in *c.* AD 875 in the River Fowey. Two further monarchs succeeded him in this Celtic kingdom.

Din Lligwy Hut Circle
Nr Moelfre, Anglesey

This Romano-British native homestead extends for over half an acre. It was principally occupied during the fourth century AD after the withdrawal of the Roman garrison on Anglesey. It consists of several rectangular buildings and two round houses, all contained within a massive defensive wall made of two lines of locally quarried limestone slabs filled in with loose stones. The rectangular buildings were used for storage and animals, while the round houses were residential. The best preserved round house has walls seven feet thick, and is twenty-one feet in diameter. Two steps lead up into the building, which quite probably was once the residence of some local powerful clan chief. Third- and fourth-century Roman coins have been excavated from the site, along with pottery and glass, and a small silver ingot.

Hadrian's Wall
Housesteads, Northumberland

The Roman Emperor Hadrian set about building a wall across the neck of Britain, eighty miles in length, in order to separate the warring Picts and Scottish tribes from Roman-occupied Britain. It runs from Tyneside in the east across the Northumberland National Park, through Cumbria, to the green pastures of the Solway Firth. Having tried and failed to conquer the whole of the country, Hadrian decided to create a barrier where no natural one existed. Construction of the wall started in AD 122 and finished six years later.

His idea was to create a barrier that would control the flow of traffic and, most importantly, prevent small groups of mounted men making profitable armed attacks on Roman Britain. Over the intervening years much of the wall has been destroyed. In places, however, most notably at Housesteads and Walltown Crags, the wall is still well preserved. Eight to ten feet wide, twelve feet tall, and on the northern side a ditch nine feet deep runs for eighty miles.

Dunnottar Castle
Nr Stonehaven, Aberdeenshire

This imposing cliff top castle is two miles south of Stonehaven. Its name, Dunnottar, implies that from early Pictish times this inaccessible rock was a fortified dun. The Celtic Christian missionary Ninian, leaving his base at the Isle of Whithorn in Dumfries and Galloway, made his way here to preach the gospel. He converted the Pictish king, and to this day the ravine that you pass through to enter the castle is known as St Ninian's Den. His holy well is nearby, though nothing now remains of his first early church. Once the stronghold of the Pictish tribe, the Mearns, it was later taken by the Pictish King Bridei, son of Bili, during the later part of the seventh century. From then until the seventeenth century it saw numerous fierce battles fought around its walls. Many interesting historical events have taken place here, among others in 1297 William Wallace burned alive an English Plantagenet garrison that was holding the castle. In 1925 a restoration programme was inaugurated by the first Lady Cowdray, and the castle that can be visited today is a direct result of those ambitious plans.

Cadbury Castle
South Cadbury, Somerset

What we now know as Cadbury Castle was first occupied in the Neolithic period, and then almost continually until the eleventh century, when it became a great cultural, probably religious and certainly military stronghold. The humble Bronze Age fort grew into an eminent Iron Age town. Four massive earthen banks, and their accompanying ditches, enclosed an almost flat, seven-hectare site. At different times inside the hillfort there were numerous buildings, including houses made of wattle, daub and thatch, a large circular building eleven metres in diameter, a bronze-smith's workshop, and a small square temple as well as large storage pits. During the Dark Ages, a large rectangular timber hall was built. A quantity of precious Mediterranean pottery and metalwork from this period has been found, implying that a wealthy, sophisticated and highly developed society existed here. Many people believe that Cadbury Castle is Arthur's Camelot, and it was from here that he led his troops to the final victory of Mount Badon.

Arthur's Castle
Tintagel, Cornwall

Arthur's Castle is an enigma situated precariously on the fortress island, with the later medieval ruins situated on the headland. No evidence of Iron Age or earlier Celtic occupation has been found here. However, large quantities of excavated pottery from what we know as the Dark Ages have been found: huge metre-high jars from Tunisia; fine red dishes from Carthage, and amphoras for wine from the Greek islands. Other pieces of pottery excavated here came from North Africa. These would all have arrived containing luxury items and were probably traded for tin. This suggests that the people who occupied Tintagel Castle during this period were important, wealthy and sophisticated, and possibly this was the seat of the high kings of Dumnonia. Since those times, there has been much rebuilding.

The Arthurian association was first established by Geoffrey of Monmouth in 1139, writing 500 years after Arthur's time, he developed the romantic fictional idea of King Arthur being the heir to the seducer King Uther Pendragon.

King Arthur's Grave
Slaughterbridge, Nr Camelford, Cornwall

According to legend, King Arthur fought his last battle at Camlann, where he received a mortal blow. He and Sir Bedivere according to Malory were the only two survivors. Some believe this to be at Slaughterbridge, a few miles inland from King Arthur's Castle at Tintagel, just north of Camelford on the River Camel.

This huge nine-foot-long, moss-and-lichen-covered stone now lies upstream from the ancient bridge on the west bank, and was once used as a stepping stone across the infant River Camel. Its inscription, both in Latin and in faint Ogham writing, is sixth or seventh century, and reads: *Latini ic iacit filivs magari* (Latinus lies here, son of Magarus). Due to a misreading, this memorial was thought to commemorate and mark the legendary place of King Arthur's death in the adjoining water meadow. However, it is far more likely to be a monument to another Celtic chieftain, perhaps slain in the battle of AD 825 fought between the Saxons and the Cornish.

Dozmary Pool
Bodmin Moor, Cornwall

Dozmary, dark and rippled, a mile-long sheet of water high on Bodmin Moor, is a teardrop-shaped pool where Excalibur, the sword that Arthur was given by the Lady of the Lake, now rests. After he was mortally wounded at Camlann, Arthur commanded Sir Bedivere to fling Excalibur into the lake. Disobeying, he hid it and on his return King Arthur asked what he had seen. Bedivere replied and by his words 'waves and wind', Arthur knew he was lying. Finally he did as commanded. A woman's hand appeared, caught it, and held Excalibur aloft before drawing it under the water. According to legend, its scabbard prevented the wearer from losing any blood in battle. But strangely not in the case of King Arthur.

Linguistically, Excalibur can be traced through the Welsh language to the Irish Caladbolg, which was the name given to the swords that Irish heroes carried into battle.

St Michael's Church
Glastonbury Tor, Somerset

Glastonbury Tor is, according to legend, Avalon. The Tor is topped by the ruins of the medieval St Michael's Church. King Arthur was taken here, according to Geoffrey of Monmouth, after his last battle. His grave was supposedly found in Glastonbury by the monks of the abbey, who were probably put up to this, at least according to Gerald of Wales, the twelfth-century chronicler. Gerald considered that Henry needed to scotch nationalistic rumours that Arthur was returning to liberate the Welsh. Others speculate that the abbot and monks perpetuated this hoax to stimulate a pilgrimage interest, and thus create the funds needed to rebuild the abbey after a disastrous fire gutted the buildings and destroyed many of its treasures.

The Tor is now in care of the National Trust and the terracing (strip lynchets) used for cultivation during the medieval period are still clearly visible. The original church was dedicated to St Michael of Torre, and was destroyed by an earthquake in 1275. After the last Abbot of Glastonbury, Richard Whiting, and two of his monks were hanged on the Tor in 1539, the church was probably abandoned and fell into ruin.

Avalon
Glastonbury Tor, Somerset

According to legend, the Isle of Avalon lies below and beyond Glastonbury Tor, now more commonly known as the Somerset Levels. According to legend, Avalon is the Celtic paradise, rich in fruits and crops, that needed no cultivation. Geoffrey of Monmouth writes that King Arthur was brought here 'mortally wounded' from his last battle at Camlann, dying on a barge accompanied by weeping fairies. Avalon is associated with this Celtic mythological 'otherworld' in the Arthurian legends. Arthur made a raid on the 'otherworld' to capture a magic cauldron kept safe by nine sorceress-queens, who were able to transform themselves into animals. It was here that the Celtic God Gwyn-ap-nudd made his kingdom of Annfwn and later was to become the fairy king. In a further legend, he met the sixth-century wandering saint, Collen (who had given his name to Llangollen).

In prehistory this area was certainly a watery marshland – an Iron Age lake village at the foot of the Tor was probably in use until after the Roman occupation and was then abandoned due to a rise in water level.

The King's Cave
Nr Blackwaterfoot, Isle of Arran, North Ayrshire

The King's Cave is one of eleven caves created by the action of the sea on the soft red sandstone. They lie in the shadow of Drumadoon Iron Age hillfort, and can be reached by the coastal path around Drumadoon Point. The King's Cave is 120 feet in length and thirty feet across, and it is shaped like the inverted wooden hull of a sailing boat. The caves, according to legend, were used by early Celtic Christians. Incised on the walls of the King's Cave, and difficult to see among the modern graffiti, are both Celtic and Pictish symbols: a broad sword cross, a horse, deer, and some concentric circles. There are examples of Ogham writing (a script in which the letters of the Roman alphabet are represented by short strokes). A rough stone seat has been chipped out of the cave face.

The King's Cave is where Robert the Bruce hid and campaigned from to attain the Scottish Crown. His fondness for this green and mountainous gem of an island was such that, in time, he was to form an honour guard from the men of Arran.

St Ninian's Cave
Isle of Whithorn, Dumfries and Galloway

St Ninian's Cave is to be found about two miles south of this sleepy coastal town, and it is here that this Celtic holy man is reputed to have spent much time in meditation.

He was a contemporary of St Patrick. However, unlike Patrick, comparatively little is known about him. Legend says he was the son of a king of Cumbria, while another account of his life claims that his mother was a Spanish princess. He travelled to Rome and on his return, when he was in his mid thirties, he visited St Martin de Tours. Impressed with what he learned from Martin, and his monks' simple way of life, he set up his own monastic settlement and school based on what he had seen in France. Soon his fame and teaching spread. He named his first church after Martin de Tours, Candida Casa, meaning 'bright shining place', which was later translated as 'whitehorn'!

Each 16 September, or on the nearest Sunday, hundreds of pilgrims follow in the saint's footsteps and walk from the Isle of Whithorn to a service of dedication held in his cave.

The Manse Pictish Standing Stone
Glamis, Angus

This beautiful half-Christian, half-pagan Pictish stone is found in the garden of the manse next to St Fergus's Kirk.

After their conversion to Christianity by missionaries, the Picts still maintained their traditions of design and stone carving. They did not produce freestanding crosses of the type being erected elsewhere, but from the seventh and eighth century started to incorporate both elements of their religion in their carving. The St Fergus Manse Cross Slab is an excellent example of both the old and the new religions. The front of this large slab has been 'dressed', and a typical Celtic cross carved in it surrounded by traditional Pictish motifs that we still do not fully understand. On the reverse of the slab, which is undressed, three symbols, typical of Pictish design, have been retained – a serpent, a fish and a mirror symbol. It has been suggested that these are probably much older than the Celtic cross on the front.

These stones, of which there are many, were probably used as devotional stones, and were positioned on trackways as a focus for prayer.

Pictish Symbols
Glamis, Angus

The name Picti was first recorded in Latin in AD 297. At that time, and before, these people were known to have covered their bodies with tattoos and woad, they were the 'painted people'. When Bede wrote seven centuries later about the Picts, no mention was made of this custom. It has been suggested that, with the passage of time, the symbols of rank adorning these people may well have been transferred to stone to commemorate an individual in death, indicating their rank, sub-tribe and name. There are about fifty different and recognizable designs, which include mirrors, combs, hammers and swords. Others are abstract designs: Z-rods, V-rods and crescents. Animals such as fish, eagles and snakes also proliferate. The Glamis Manse Stone is one of many Pictish carved symbol stones. Most still *in situ* are in the Moray, Aberdeenshire and Highland regions, however, few are as interestingly carved and in such good condition, and show the change from a pagan tradition to a Christian one. Today, though, the meanings of these carvings can only be surmised.

Iona
Argyll and Bute, Strathclyde

The long journey to reach the small and remote island of Iona, a ten-minute ferry journey across the Sound of Iona from Fionnphort on the rugged and beautiful Island of Mull, is made each year by thousands of pilgrims, and has been for 1,500 years. For today's pilgrims, the remoteness of this exquisite place gives a tremendous sense of spiritual isolation and distance from the material and twentieth-century world that they have left, perhaps only fleetingly, behind.

Long before Columba first visited Iona with a group of twelve companions in AD 563, the island had been a place of religious learning. The Druids are supposed to have journeyed here to elude persecution by the Roman armies. In AD 410, Fergus II of Scotland formed a treaty with Alaric the Goth, and after the plunder of Rome, he added to the library already in existence on Iona.

Today the island is principally owned by the National Trust of Scotland and the Iona Community. It boasts the beautifully restored abbey, St Oran's Chapel, The Nunnery and a wealth of Celtic crosses. The solitude and the dramatic and bracing climate are an experience of a lifetime.

Loch Scridain
Isle of Mull, Argyll and Bute, Strathclyde

When Columba left Ireland for Iona with his twelve companions, the island would not have been considered a different country from Ireland. The land was covered with thick forests and was, in places, almost impossible to pass. The easiest and most direct route almost anywhere was by water. These evangelists travelled in light boats – coracles – carrying them on their backs when necessary from one loch to another.

Shortly after establishing the Iona community, Columba felt threatened by the advances that the heathen King Brude of the Picts had made from his base on the east coast, where Inverness is now. Brude had extended his territory as far as Dalriada, so Iona could be taken at any time. Columba and a group of emissaries travelled across Scotland to meet with King Brude. Historians do not know the exact role that Columba played in those meetings. However, Brude was converted to Christianity in AD 565 and confirmed the Iona community's safety.

St Columba's Chapel
Iona, Argyll and Bute

When Columba arrived in Iona from Ireland in AD 563, the island, though remote, would have seemed an accessible and hospitable place to set up a religious community. The land was covered with deciduous trees, the pastures fertile and the sea plentiful. Nothing now remains of the original church, but just to the north of the chapel is Torr an Aba, a small rocky knoll where Columba undoubtedly made his cell. The chapel is ninth or tenth century. Originally this chapel would have held a relic of the saint and his venerated bones. Due to the murderous attacks on this religious community by blood-lustful Vikings, these precious items were eventually moved for safety to Kells, in County Meath, Ireland, probably sometime during the Dark Ages. Outside the chapel is a replica of St John's Cross – the original, now fragmented, is on view in the museum along with numerous other examples of Iona stone craftsmanship.

St Oran's Chapel and the Reilig Odhrain
Iona, Argyll and Bute

St Oran of Letteragh in Ireland, founded a Christian community and cemetery that was to become know as the Reilig Odhrain, the 'Royal Burial Ground', on Iona some twenty years before Columba arrived with his twelve followers in AD 563. Columba thought of himself according to some sources as Christ's Druid, as did St Patrick, and there is a gruesome legend that Oran sacrificed himself, to be entombed alive in the foundations of Columba's new church.

St Oran's restored chapel is the earliest of the three religious buildings on the island. The doorway is the most interesting feature: the middle row of the rounded decorative stonework is carved with a series of, now much denuded, heads.

In 1549 Iona was visited by Donald Monroe, the Dean of the Isles, who reported that forty-eight Scottish and twelve Irish, Norwegian and French kings were buried there, along with many West Highland and Hebridean chiefs.

Celtic Crosses
Iona, Argyll and Bute, Strathclyde

St Martin's Cross and the Maclean's Cross are both extremely fine examples of the Celtic cross style. St Martin's Cross is the older of the two and has been dated to the second half of the eighth century. From its base it stands seventeen feet tall, and its two arms include slots that may well once have held either wooden or metal extensions, thus altering the proportions that are familiar to us today. Close Christian links between Ireland and Iona, and Iona's isolation, led to a distinctive style of high cross design. However, this stone originally came from mid-Argyll and it has been suggested that the stone mason may well, therefore, have come from Pictland where this motif was well developed.

The Maclean's Cross is the tallest freestanding cross on Iona, and is furthest from the abbey. It is of the late Iona school of cross design. The west face shows the crucifixion while the east face is carved in a complicated Celtic interlacing pattern.

St Credan's Celtic Cross
Sancreed Parish Church, Cornwall

Sancreed Parish Church is dedicated to St Credan – which St Credan, however, is open to speculation. St Credan, disciple of St Petrock, whose body now lies in Bodmin, or St Credan, son of Illadham, who eventually returned to his native Ireland to settle in County Wicklow?

The present church dates from the thirteenth century. However, the circular configuration of the site suggests that the church was established on a much older monastic site. Sancreed Holy Well is close by and would give credence to this theory.

There are five Celtic crosses in the churchyard. The nine-feet-tall, wheel-headed cross adjacent to the old diagonal path leading to the church is probably the best example of its kind in Cornwall. All four sides of the cross are inscribed and the bold relief is of a robed and crucified figure of Christ.

St Cuthbert's Caves
Nr Holy Island, Northumberland

Cuthbert as a young shepherd had a vision on the night of Aidan's death, as a result of which he joined the Celtic Church. As a young missionary under the Abbot Eata, he transferred to Lindisfarne, where he lived as a hermit, first on St Cuthbert's Island and then on Inner Farne Island. He built a cell there and stayed alone for nine years. He eventually agreed to succeed Eata in AD 685, and set about embracing his new life. He was old and not strong, and after two years he moved back to Farne Island to die. His body was returned to Lindisfarne in AD 687. Eleven years later his remains were exhumed to be enshrined in a small silver cask. Astonishingly, his body had not decomposed, word spread of this 'miracle' and Lindisfarne became a pilgrimage centre. Towards the end of the eighth century, for fear of Viking raiding parties, it was decided to remove his body and many other holy relics to Durham Cathedral, where they remain to this day. The monks rested for some time in these natural sandstone caves, which have since then been known and visited by pilgrims as St Cuthbert's Caves.

Lindisfarne Priory
Holy Island, Northumberland

Lindisfarne has been a centre of Christianity since AD 635, when Aidan, an Irish monk, was summoned by the Saxon King Oswald of Northumbria to be the first missionary bishop of Bernicia. Oswald had known Aidan when he and his brothers and sister were living as royal refugees on Iona, having fled there when their father, King Aethelfrith, had lost his throne and kingdom to the pagan Edwin. On his father's death in battle, Oswald, who had been baptized a Christian on Iona, took back the throne and sent for a group of Celtic Christian missionaries to re-evangelize his lands.

Aidan led these men and eventually settled his community on the island of Inis Medcoit, which became known as Lindisfarne – later to be called Holy Island. Lindisfarne excelled as a Celtic centre of culture and learning for more than 200 years. Nothing now remains of the first church that was built after Aidan's death in AD 651. During the eighth century, Holy Island was taken by the Vikings and then was re-established as a religious community during the twelfth century. The ruined priory is all that now remains of these events.

Runes, Maes Howe
Nr Stromnes, Orkney

Runic writing is one of the earliest forms of alphabet and it was used by Scandinavian peoples. This example is within the great Maes Howe Burial Chamber, described as one of the wonders of the prehistoric world. Broken into centuries ago by a Viking plundering party, they left a series of twenty-four inscriptions. The Runic graffiti once translated is, in many cases, no different from what you can read anywhere in a modern city today. It boasts of female conquests and the theft by Hakon who 'single-handed bore treasure from this howe'.

Up-Helly-Aa
Lerwick, Shetland

'Deliver us O Lord from the wrath of the Viking.' So wrote a Celtic monk in his monastery. It was the rich treasure that the monasteries had accumulated that these heathen and murderous seafarers were greedy for. They came in their longships during the latter part of the eighth century, raped and pillaged wherever they landed, and shook the Celtic Christian civilization to its very core with their almost unbelievable acts of cruelty. Typical of their practice was the custom of 'blood-eagling': Earl Einar cut a bloody eagle into his enemies back by placing a sword on his victims spine and hacking all the ribs away. He then pulled out the lungs and offered them as a gesture of thanks to Odin, the chief of the gods and Lord of the Runes. In time, they settled much of Celtic Scotland – the Highlands and the Islands. It was not until 1469 that Shetland became British. Each year Shetlanders in Lerwick, and in other small island communities, celebrate their Viking ancestry with a spectacular fire festival. A huge Viking longship is hauled through the teeming streets of Lerwick in a torchlit procession, the festivities culminating with the boat being fired.

St Illtud's or Samson's Cross
St Illtud's Church, Llanwit Major, Vale of Glamorgan

The west church at Llanwit Major stands on one of the oldest Celtic Christian sites in Britain. St Illtud was probably a Breton, converted as a young man to Christianity, and travelled to Wales in about AD 500.

What little we know of him comes from a book, *The Life of St Samson of Dol*, written in about AD 610, around a hundred years after his death. Samson was one of Illtud's students and followed him as abbot at this monastery, which claims to be the first centre of learning in Britain and some say the first 'university'. Nothing now remains of this church, save for the dedication stones. The cross in the foreground is St Illtud's or Samson's Cross, which may have once been capped by a wheel cross. It was found buried in the grounds to the north of the church, and when it was dug up two skeletons were found to be buried beneath it.

Celtic Grave Slab
The Church of St Tysilio and St Mary, Meifod, Powys

According to legend, when St Gwyddfarch was asked in AD 550 where he wanted his first church to be built, he replied in Welsh, *'yma y mae i fod'* (here it is to be). Hence the name of this attractive farming community – Meifod. His body is buried according to legend at the top of Allt-yr-Ancr (Anchorite's Hill), which is a short way out of the village at a place known as Gwely Gwyddfarch – the bed of Gwyddfarch. During the ninth century, Mathrafal became the chief residence of the princes of Powys, and Meifod the religious centre for the area. The Celtic grave slab is thought to be a memorial to one of those princes. It was discovered during the last century, and was described by the then vicar of Meifod in his book, *The History of the Diocese of St Asaph*, as 'a fine Celtic coffin lid, ornamented at the head with a crucifix within a circle, and a cross below it and around its borders with curious interlacing but no inscription . . . along the outer edges are serpents and representations of evil, nearer in are the triquetra, the cross and the crown, down the centre a Latin cross and at the head a Greek crucifix with stigmata, the whole emblematic of the conquest of sin'.

St David's Head, Coetan Arthur and Ramsey Island, and Hut Circles
St David's Head, St David's Pembrokeshire

This wild and inhospitable headland was once the home of the Iron Age Demetae tribe. The site was excavated in the nineteenth century and a few spindle whorls, pottery and beads were found. There are seven hut circles that are situated at the very tip of this rocky, sheer-faced promontory, cut off and lying behind two outer ditches and what was once a massive, dry stone wall (twelve feet tall and nine feet wide).

The area has many prehistoric monuments, Coetan Arthur, a now denuded Neolithic burial chamber, is on high land overlooking the Demetae tribesmen's promontory fort, and near this ancient place there can still be seen the remains of an Iron Age field pattern system. Two further Neolithic burial chambers near the summit of Carn Llidi Bychan look down on the whole tribal farming settlement and out towards Ramsey Island. This island was once the home of the sixth-century Celt St Justinian, a holy man from Brittany and a great friend and companion of St David. According to legend he was murdered by his servant, and rising from the dead he walked across Ramsey Sound to the mainland carrying his head under his arm.

St Non's Chapel
St David's, Pembrokeshire

St Non was the mother of St David and, according to tradition, she was of noble birth, a religious woman and, at some time in her life, a nun. She gave birth to St David during the first half of the sixth century in a house in what is now known as Whitewell Field, on the edge of the cliffs overlooking Skoder Island. There were some small standing stones nearby indicating that this place was quite probably once a Bronze Age settlement. An inscribed seventh-century cross was dug up in the field and it now sits in the ruined chapel marking St David's birthplace.

Not far away is St Non's Well, said to have sprung up during a thunderstorm on the night of St David's birth. St Non's Chapel, next to St Non's Sanctuary, was built in 1934 using stones from dilapidated cottages in Whitewell Field, which in turn had been built with stones from the church buildings that had grown up around St David's birthplace. The serene and simple chapel contains, among others, a stained glass window in the style of William Morris showing St Non and David arriving by boat in Brittany. There is also a window dedicated to the Celtic saint St Winefride.

St David's Cathedral
St David's, Pembrokeshire

David's father was Sant, a Prince of Ceredigiona. Educated in the ways of the Celtic Church from infancy, his principal tutors were Illtud and Paulinus, whose sight was restored when David performed his first miracle. Returning home, David founded a monastery at Vallis Rosina, 'The Valley of the Little Marsh'. The present Norman cathedral was built on the spot where this first early church stood.

David was one of the most heroic of all the Celtic holy men, and monastic life under him was particularly difficult. His monks were expected to spend much of their time in solitude and prayer, as well as share in hard manual labour: 'they placed yoke on their own shoulders' rather than use oxen. Their clothes were made of animal skins and all property was held in common. Their diet consisted of bread and herbs, seasoned with salt, as well as wild leeks – now the national emblem of Wales. 'David the Waterman', as he was also known, spent many hours in prayer standing in water to subdue the flesh. He died on 1 March, probably in 589, now commemorated by the Welsh as St David's Day.

St Govan's Chapel
Nr Bosherton, Pembrokeshire

During the fifth and sixth centuries, there was much movement of Christian missionaries. They often lived as hermits, setting up cells and preaching the new religion of Christianity.

St Govan is thought to have been St Gobham, the Abbot of Dairinis, of County Wexford in Ireland. According to legend he was pursued across the Irish Sea by pirates. On reaching the cliffs of Pembrokeshire, a fissure in the rock opened up and enclosed him, opening and releasing him only after the marauders had left. St Govan subsequently built his hermitage along with a well where he had found safety.

The present building is from the eleventh century, though it is thought to have been built on the foundations of the original cell. There is an altar at the east end that is reputed to contain St Govan's remains. Immediately behind the altar, steps lead to a small cell and off that there is a vertical cleft in the rock, which, to this day, bears the impression of St Govan's body.

Caldey Island
Nr Tenby, Pembrokeshire

Caldey Island is two and a half miles by motorboat from the busy and ever-popular seaside town of Tenby. A tranquil place, Caldey Island has been a centre of Celtic Christian learning since at least the sixth century, when a monastery was founded by the monks from Llanwit Major. The island was first mentioned in *The Life of St Samson of Dol*, a story written in the seventh century. Caldey's first abbot was Pyro, who worked with his hands all day, but one night in a drunken stupor he fell and drowned in the monastery well.

The island is now inhabited by fifteen 'silent' Cistercian monks who try to continue the work of St Benedict's Rule, '. . . of joy in God's beauty, and in the simplicity of life'. Caldey Island is a self-supporting community of sixty farmers, boatmen, teachers and children, producing perfume, chocolate and other goods that are sold in the island shop and in Tenby. The monks live a peaceful life, farming 300 acres, working in the kitchens, maintaining their buildings and generally assisting in various tourist projects.

Pilgrims' Cross
Nevern, Pembrokeshire

No longer than a foot in length, this Pilgrims' Cross is carved into the cliff face along an ancient route through a wood, a quarter of a mile from Nevern church-yard. It is positioned immediately above a small, seat-like hollow in the cliff that may once have been a shrine for pilgrims journeying to St David's from Holywell. In more recent times, pilgrims face the cliff, kneel in the hollow, touch the cross and pray.

The church at Nevern is dedicated to an Irish monk, St Brynach – a contemporary of St David, the patron saint of Wales, who in the sixth century founded this church in an isolated wooded area. There are still many early Christian relics here. The Great Cross is a huge and beautifully preserved Celtic monument reputed to have been carried and put in place by St David. In and outside this magnificent church there are also two other Celtic memorial stones, both inscribed in Latin and Ogham.

Tarr Steps
Nr Winsford, Exmoor, Somerset

Tarr Steps, the ancient 'clapper' bridge spanning the River Barle, is reputed to be the oldest bridge in Britain. It is of dry stone construction and is made up of seventeen spans crossing fifty-three metres of the river, which runs off Exmoor through an ancient wooded landscape. There is no evidence of Bronze Age construction, but there are numerous Bronze Age tracks that converge on Tarr Steps, which derives its name from the Celtic word *tochar*, meaning 'causeway'. During the Dark Ages it may well have been used by Celtic pilgrims journeying from one religious centre to another. Legend has it that the Devil constructed Tarr Steps as a place to sunbathe, and vowed to destroy any person who tried to cross them. A parson was sent to confront the Devil, and on meeting him, the parson was cursed and cussed, and foully abused. The parson gave back as good as he got, and so impressed the Devil that the Tarr Steps were conceded. But beware, the Devil still has the sunbathing rights!

Bardsey Island
Nr Aberdaron, Gwynedd

Since at least the sixth century, Bardsey Island or, in Welsh, Ynys Enlli, lying two miles off the coast of the Lleyn Peninsular has been a place of Celtic pilgrimage. In medieval times, three pilgrimages across the rough and perilous Bardsey Sound were considered as good as one journey to Rome.

In AD 607, King Ethelfrid, king of Bernicia, massacred 1,200 monks at Bangor-is-y-Doed. The remaining monks – over a thousand of them – fled the pagan warlord to Bardsey Island for safety , and since then this island has been known as the Island of the Saints. St Cadfan founded a monastery here in AD 516, and in the 13th century an Augustine Abbey dedicated to St Mary, which is now in ruin, was built on the same site.

During the medieval period, the misreading of a 1,000 year old memorial stone to 'an old and wise priest' led to a popular legend that over 20,000 saints were buried on this tiny windswept island.

St Cwyfan's Church
The Old Church of Llangwyfan, Nr Aberffraw, Anglesey

This medieval church is dedicated to the Irish saint whose base was at Glendalough, not far from a stretch of the Irish coast that stands opposite Llangwyfan. In medieval times, Llangwyfan was a prosperous and populous area and the church was built on an islet between two brooks. Over the centuries, however, the land was eroded and has become an island – and Llangwyfan has depopulated. Now known as the 'church in the sea', its lan is only 100 yards across, built on what has now become a rocky outcrop in Caernarfon Bay, which can be reached at low tide across a causeway of boulders. The Rev. John Skinner wrote in 1802: 'Llangwyfan church is erected on a rocky peninsula jutting out into the sea and is an island at high water so that not infrequently the congregation are interrupted in their devotion by the rapid approach of the waves.' Services were held here until a new church was built in 1872. The old church is still sometimes used – depending on the tide.

St Seirol's Well and Puffin Island
Penmon, Anglesey

After the expulsion of the Irish from Anglesey, a period of relative peace ensued. St Seirol and St Cybi were Celtic holy men, and colleagues who both came under the patronage of the Christian King Maelgwn Gwynedd, whose power base for ruling north Wales was at Aberffraw on Anglesey.

St Seirol made his first Celtic Christian centre at Penmon. His holy well, where he performed baptisms, and his hut circle (rebuilt during the eighteenth century) are now adjacent to Penmon Priory.

Nearby on Puffin Island, known also as Ynys Seirol and, during the Norse period, as Priestholm, is where St Seirol founded his monastery. Gerald of Wales in his journal of 1158 described it as '. . . the ecclesiastical island, because many bodies of saints are deposited there and no woman is suffered to enter it'.

Little now remains on Puffin Island. It is St Seirol's and his patron's, Maelgwn Gwynedd, last resting place and the monastery is now in ruin.

St Germoe's Chair
Germoe, Cornwall

This ancient church is dedicated to the Irish king and missionary Germochus, or Germoe. He and his sister, St Breaca, who gave her name to the nearby village of Breage, were Irish missionaries who came to Cornwall during the Dark Ages. According to legend they escaped with their lives from the local heathen chief Teudar, and travelled up the River Hayle to the hill known as Tregonning.

Germoe elected to make his lan in the wooded valley to the south-west, but nothing now remains of his first church. The present church dates from the twelfth century. Within the church the ancient font is carved with a mysterious Celtic head, which is thought to have come from the first church. In the churchyard is the unexplained, so-called St Germoe's Chair. There has been much speculation regarding its origin and intended use. According to Canon Coulthard in his book on the parish, it may well have something to do with Palm Sunday celebration in the medieval Church. Alternatively, it could also be a symbol of authority, while others believe that St Germoe may have been buried beneath it.

St Nectan's Waterfall
Nr Boscastle, Cornwall

St Nectan's Waterfall was immortalized in Maclise's painting 'Girl at the Waterfall', once owned by Charles Dickens and now hanging in the Victoria and Albert Museum in London. The waterfall, though not large – the drop is only about sixty feet – is quite beautiful. The unusual geology has created at least four *kieves* (Cornish for basins), the water cascading through one to another.

St Nectan was a sixth-century Welsh saint who settled here in about AD 500. The son of St Brychan, he was a hermit who built his baptistery on the banks of the River Trevillitt, at the summit of the falls. He was killed by pagan robbers and, after his death, his shrine in Hartland, Devon became a focus for pilgrimages for many years.

This remote and densely wooded place has many legends associated with it. St Nectan was supposed to have had a huge silver bell, which he rang to warn sailors of the danger they faced from the treacherous cliffs along this coast. He eventually decided that no non-believer should ever hear the ring of the silver bell and dropped it into the waterfall. Occasionally, it may still be possible to hear it ring; an omen of bad luck.

St Gwenfaen's Well
Rhoscolyn, Anglesey

St Gwenfaen was the daughter of Paul Hen, and the sister to St Peulan. She was one of a number of sixth-century Celtic saints active in Anglesey. They were religious devotees known as the Colidei, who lived as hermits – others in their number were Cybi, Tysilio, and Donwenna. Her well is an excellent example of an early Celtic Christian religious structure. Situated overlooking the sea at Rhoscolyn headland, it is almost entirely below ground level. It comprises three stone-lined chambers. At the entrance, three steps lead to the first chamber, which contains four corner seats. The second chamber contains the well, now only a foot deep. The third area is reached down four steps and leads to the overflow well water.

St Gwenfaen's Well water is reputed to have been able to cure mental illness and to foretell the future depending on the way the bubbles rose after two white stones were cast into it.

St Cybi's Holy Well
Llangybi, Caernarfon, Gwynedd

St Cybi was a sixth-century saint who founded this holy well and the church nearby.

There are several buildings that are all now quite ruined. The main well chamber is possibly twelfth century, though its foundation no doubt stretches back to St Cybi's time. The actual holy well is behind the well chamber, which is built of massively thick stone walls. Sunk into the wall are five stone seats, and steps lead down into the bathing water, which is fed by the Holy Well.

The holy well was renowned for its healing properties and it was famous for being able to cure warts, lameness, blindness and rheumatism. A cure was affected by drinking equal quantities of well water and sea water over a prescribed period, followed by bathing in the well chamber, and then retiring to the adjoining cottage to wait.

According to some accounts, the guardian spirit of St Cybi's Well was embodied in a sacred eel. If it coiled around a patient's leg during treatment in the water, a cure could be predicted. However, when the eel was removed from the waters, pilgrims believed that the well's power to heal was dissipated.

Madron Chapel and Well
Madron, Cornwall

This serene and delightful Celtic place is 200 yards down an overgrown and narrow path, between a high hedge and a copse, a mile north of the village of Madron, named after its saint St Maddern.

Votive offerings hang from the small thorn tree that marks the site of the well, whose water is said to cure rickets and assist in divination. Forty yards further on are the remains of St Maddern's Cell, surrounded by an overgrown and ruined medieval enclosure. Said to have been dismantled by Puritan soldiers in 1646, this tranquil cell is still, on occasion, used by pilgrims for services and baptisms. At one end is a granite slab, which acts as an altar, and at the other end is a font, or basin, through which water flows. Here, over a thousand years ago St Maddern first baptized villagers. His feast day is remembered on 17 May.

Holy Well, St Anne's Church
Whitstone, Cornwall

In Celtic mythology Anu, the great Mother goddess, was associated with the land. On a high ridge north-west of the farming community of Whitstone is the village church, dedicated to St Anne, a popular saint in fourteenth-century Cornwall, and by repute the mother of the Blessed Virgin.

Inside this serene, medieval church, which was almost completely 'restored' by over-zealous Victorians, a pagan Celtic legacy remains. There has been a church near this spot since Celtic pagan times.

Built into the foundations, and to the right of the porch as you enter, is a sparkling, quartz-like 'White stone' believed to be of pagan origin, and possibly a pagan altar. This stone gives Whitstone its name. In a lower corner of the churchyard, St Anne's Holy Well can be found. Modernized by the Victorians, it is now unfortunately without its bronze statue of St Anne. This Holy Well is undoubtedly very ancient, and may once have been used by early Celtic saints. Within the Holy Well, on the rear wall, is a primitive carving of a head above a niche that once, almost certainly, would have been used to accept offerings to this pagan deity.

Coffin Well, Tissington Well Dressing
Tissington, Derbyshire

The history of well dressing can be traced back for over 2,000 years to the pagan Celtic cult, when powerful deities were thought to live in the water. With the arrival of Christianity many of these wells were recon-secrated and given Christian names. In Derbyshire, where well dressing is most widely prac-tised, the celebration of what was once a pagan cult is now part of the Christian calendar. Well dressing at Tissington was first mentioned in 1758 by the clerk to the House of Commons, Nicholas Hardinge, who wrote that he saw at Tissington: 'Springs adorned with garlands in honour of these fountains which are annually commemo-rated on Holy Thursday.'

Now, six wells at Tissington are dressed by the villagers for Ascension Day. In the morning a church service is held. This is followed by a procession led by the clergy, where each of the wells is blessed in turn.

St Beuno's Church
Culbone, Nr Porlock Weir, Somerset

St Beuno was born in Powys in the sixth century and during his lifetime founded several monasteries from his base at Caerwnt, a Roman town near Chepstow. What his actual connection with Culbone was is difficult to say. However, the area is rich in prehistoric and Celtic sites. The Dark Age standing stone on the hills above Culbone, carved with a wheeled cross, was used as a directional sign, which indicates that this little, isolated, jewel-like church was of significance as a place of pilgrimage in his time.

The body of the church is Norman, however, and the oldest part is believed to be the two light, semicircular-headed windows on the north side of the chancel, carved from a single block of sandstone. Incorporated in this is a unique and mysterious carving of a face, only just discernible, forming a kind of capital. This window is probably more than 1,000 years old and is believed to be part of St Beuno's original cell.

St Beuno's Chapel
Clynnog Fawr, Gwynedd

St Beuno was an important saint in north Wales, one of the sons of the royal family of Morgannwg. He founded this church at Clynnog Fawr in the sixth century on land given to him by the King of Gwynedd, Cadwallon. St Bueno died on 21 April, AD 642. The present church is fifteenth century, and during excavation some years ago the remains of what appears to have been his original cell were discovered beneath the fifteen-foot passage between the main body of the church and St Beuno's Chapel.

St Beuno is best remembered today for his miraculous powers of healing, and in particular the placing of his niece Winefride's head back on her shoulders and restoring her life at Holywell.

The Shrine, Shrewsbury Abbey
Shrewsbury, Shropshire

This medieval carving, now displayed in The Abbey Church of St Peter and St Paul, probably shows, from left to right, John the Baptist, St Winefride and St Beuno. It was found in 1933 in the grounds of the Swan Hotel and comes from St Winefride's shrine.

According to tradition, Winefride was the beautiful daughter of Tewyth and Gwenlo, and her uncle was St Beuno. Caradoc, a chieftain from Hawarden, on returning from a hunting trip attempted to rape her. She fled to her uncle's cell for safety. Caradoc gave chase, and in his rage he drew his sword and sliced off her head. Beuno on hearing the commotion came out of his cell and placed Winefride's head back on her body. Her life was restored. Legend has it that where her head fell a spring of water gushed forth, producing the Holy Well that gives Holywell its name. Winefride became a nun, and then Abbess of Gwytherin. Her relics were moved to Shrewsbury in 1138. In 1550, with the dissolution of the monasteries, her shrine was desecrated and her bones scattered. Only one finger bone survived, half being kept at Shrewsbury the other returned to Holywell.

St Winefride's Shrine
Holywell, Flintshire

Winefride was born in the sixth century, the daughter of Tewyth and Gwenlo, and her uncle was St Beuno. After Caradoc's murderous attack on her, and her miraculous restoration to life, she became a nun, and eventually an abbess. Her remaining relics were eventually returned to Holywell in 1852.

Holywell was once one of the most important pilgrimage sites in Britain, and even today thousands of pilgrims travel there each year to take the water and pray for a cure. Thus, St Winefride's Well is the oldest shrine of unbroken pilgrimage in Britain. From Whitsuntide to the end of September, pilgrims are given the opportunity to venerate the saint's relics – the little portion of St Winefride's finger bone. St Winefride is honoured with two feast days – 22 June (the date of her miraculous restoration to life) and 3 November (the date of her death). The medieval statue of St Winefride in the Holy Well shows the raised scar surrounding her neck where, in life, her head had been restored.

CONTEMPORARY CELTS

Celtic Fertility Figure
The Church of St James the Great, Abson, Somerset

The church of St James the Great has been a place of Christian worship since the twelfth century. By AD 950, the Hundred of Pucklechurch, in which the church stands, had been granted by the Crown to the abbey of Glastonbury. This was no doubt as part of the 'soul-scot' paid to the abbey because of the burial in its grounds of King Edmund, who had been murdered in Pucklechurch in AD 946.

High on the east wall is the remarkably well-preserved and clearly defined rampant male Celtic fertility figure, more than two feet long. The east end of the church had fallen into decay by the sixteenth century and was rebuilt, and it may well be that this figure was added then. It is possible that during the Victorian period it was covered so as not to offend, only to be revealed recently during renovations. According to the church leaflet this figure is 'a demon' who may have lost his tail.

He told me his name was Reg Boulton and that his family had lived in the village since at least 1670. The first Boulton had died, unmarried, leaving a son and 'without wood', which meant, he said, that she had been a pauper. Laughing and obviously proud, he told me his family had 'come a long way since those days'. Mr Boulton had never 'slept out of the village' except during the war, and had spent his earlier life as a banker mason. I enquired what exactly that meant. 'It was a man who worked at a stone bench. I did carving. I'm not clever enough to create but I can copy anything,' he explained. Looking up at the carving on the north wall of the church, I asked him what it was and if he knew anything about it. 'It's a fertility witch, I've done three of them in my time, I don't know what they were mind you. He'd [the architect] bring in a drawing, sometimes a plaster cast and I would do one in a day. It was always considered a bit of a joke, I'd have to make all the bits a woman has exaggerated.' The Sheela-na-gig that Reg Boulton was looking up at is one of about forty in Britain still *in situ* in old churches. There are over a hundred recorded in Ireland. Sheela-na-gig probably comes from the Irish *Sighle Na Geioch* meaning 'the old hag of the breasts'. They are carved usually in stone, showing a female displaying her genitalia, and were once positioned in a prominent location so that they might easily be seen and venerated. They date from the early medieval period and are thought by some authorities to represent a pre-Christian Celtic war goddess. She appears as a seductive old hag to the hero, and when he consents to make love to her, she turns into a beautiful woman. Other authorities believe that the explicit nature of the Sheela-na-gig was designed to warn off evil spirits, while others see these figures as symbols of fertility. Many have been destroyed by puritanical church authorities or so badly defaced that their explicit nature is not clear, while others have been boarded over.

These and other Celtic gods and goddesses are still visible in some churches. At Sancreed Church in Cornwall, the rood screen has numerous medieval figures of Celtic deities carved onto it – a triple-headed king, and several janiform heads all represent these deities. The Green Man figures, for example, are more numerous than Sheela-na-gigs; they, too, date from 1066 onwards. These are often horrific depictions, carved in stone and wood, of a semi-human face not attached to a body. The head is usually surrounded with vegetation that is being 'born' via the mouth. They are thought to be synonymous with the Jack-in-Green figure of May celebrations, who sometimes still accompanies Morris dance teams. Morris dancers can also be in disguise, whether it is a blackened face, as is the case of the Britannia Coconut Dancers in Bacup, who traditionally appear for the first time each year on each Easter Saturday, or the beribboned and belled handkerchief-waving dancers that are familiar today at almost all country events. The Burry Man from South Queensferry in Scotland is one such Jack-in-Green figure, a modern representation of a pre-Christian Celtic fertility inducing deity.

There are many other twentieth-century country customs that have been derived from early Celtic traditions. For example each January the Haxey Hood Game takes place in Lincolnshire. Some authorities believe that this, though much changed, may be connected to the Celtic fertility cults. As indeed is the hugely popular Padstow Hobby Horse celebration that takes place on 1 May each year. The 'Obby Oss' leaps and dances through the narrow and crowded streets of Padstow with a 'Teaser' leading it, occasionally catching a young woman under its 'black skirts'. This is taken as a good luck omen that the young girl will soon fall pregnant, or get a husband. In November the villagers of Shebbear in Devon 'turn the devil's stone'. This large one-ton megalith is believed to have been dropped by the Devil on his fall from heaven to hell, and an ill fate will befall the village unless it is turned annually. Thus, to a discordant peal on the church bells, the massive bolder is heaved over with the aid of stakes.

The Druids were prehistoric Celtic high priests, the religious leaders and learned men about whom Julius Caesar wrote when the Romans first came to Britain. During the eighteenth century, with the 'discovery' of Stonehenge and Avebury, and the interest this generated, Charles II climbed Silbury Hill and visited both sites. More than 1,500 years after the prehistoric Druids, eminent antiquarians were fostering the idea that Stonehenge and Avebury were Druid temples. John Aubrey proclaimed in 1740 that Stonehenge was: '. . . the metropolitical Church of the chief Druids of Britain. . . This was the *locus consecratus* where they met at some great festivals of the year, as well to perform the extraordinary sacrifices and religious rites, as to determine causes and civil matters.' The Neodruidic revival was born.

In 1792 Iolo Morgannwg, the eighteenth-century Welsh poet and antiquarian, started the first Gorsedd of Bards, and in order to give these Druids a feeling of greater antiquity he invented prayers and chants for the occasion and conferred bardic degrees. These Druids now officiate at the annual National Eisteddfod in Wales, which is the largest cultural gathering in Europe. Originally derived from a bardic tournament, when poets and musicians would compete against each other, the National Eisteddfod takes place over a ten-day period and attracts more than 150,000 visitors. The whole event is conducted in Welsh. There are numerous other Druidic groups functioning in Celtic Britain, ranging from those that conduct their ceremonies at Stonehenge each summer solstice to smaller, less-well-established groups. For example, the British Druid Order holds mesmeric meetings on auspicious occasions throughout the year at Avebury and other Celtic sites.

Ed Prynn and his partner Glynis, who are tucked away in St Merryn near Padstow in Cornwall, are two extraordinary, eccentric Celts. They are modern-day Druids, as Glynis says: 'He's an Archdruid, sort of self-appointed.' Ed has a mischevious sense of humour and enjoys nothing more than putting on his flowing white robes and showing visiting holidaymakers around his megalithic garden. In one corner they have a triangular 'holed' wedding stone. They conduct 'weddings' for Druid couples at the stone. Partners stand on either side holding hands, often dressed like Ed and Glynis in flowing robes, and with flowers in their hair. Glynis recites some special words: 'Above you are the stars, Below you the stones, As the time does pass, Remember . . . Like a star should your love be constant, Like a stone should your love be firm . . .' Ed, according to Glynis, says more or less what comes into his mind. 'At the end of the ceremony, it's a lovely occasion we give them a special certificate that we have had printed.' The 'marriage certificate' that Ed and Glynis give the couple certifies that the certificate relates to a 'Druid Marriage only'.

Glynis also does traditional bed and breakfast. The guest room in their home has a 'mystic' four-poster bed, which is canopied with an embroidered copy of the ancient Celtic hill carving of the Cerne Abbas Giant. This unique British carving, cut into the chalk hillside, is of a Herculean figure wielding a club. It is principally remembered, however, for its enormous erect phallus. The largest megalith in the gardens is a huge granite block. This capstone is precariously balanced on three upright stones – an almost exact copy of Cornwall's best-known Neolithic chamber tomb: Lanyon Quoit. According to legend, King Arthur took his last meal here before his final battle, and Merlin predicted that he and 'the once and future king' would meet again there before Armageddon. Ed calls this stone 'The Angle's Runway', which he considers more appropriate and in keeping with his fantasy.

Sheela-na-gigs
The Church of Amney St Peter,
Amney St Peter,
Gloucestershire and The All
Saints Church, Oaksey,
Gloucestershire

In Britain, there are probably over forty Sheela-na-gigs in existence, and there may be more still to be rediscovered. Found almost exclusively in ancient churches, these primitive carvings, usually in stone, represent a last vestige of a pre-Christian, Celtic pagan female goddess. The adornment of churches with Sheela-na-gigs dates from the fifth century to about the twelfth century. However, it can be assumed that this Celtic goddess is much older and probably she has been venerated since people first worshipped gods. The reason for the re-emergence of this deity during the Dark Ages and into the early medieval period is open to speculation.

It can be assumed that most have not survived, since their important and prominent position on churches, and their overt sexual nature, caused offence. Those that did survive Puritanism and the Victorian era did so because they were viewed as a warning against the 'sins of the flesh' or because they were covered over. Nowadays, with a more enlightened Church, these extraordinary relics of a pagan past are being cared for and preserved.

Triple-headed King and Janiform Heads
Sancreed Church, Cornwall

The parish church of Sancreed is dedicated to the Celtic saint St Credan. An ancient monastic site, the present thirteenth-century church has a superbly carved and coloured early rood screen. Hundreds of years ago, a Celtic artisan carved a series of grotesque images, including wild mysterious beasts and at least three janiform heads, which look into the future and to the past at the same time. One triple head of a king next to a wild beast is also represented. In Celtic mythology, the head was symbolic of power, knowledge and divine persona. The more heads, the more powerful the god. The iconography has parallels with the Christian Trinity: God the Father, God the Son and God the Holy Spirit.

Green Man
St Andrew's Church, South Tawton, Devon

The profusion and tremendous popularity of the Green Man, which is a Celtic symbol of vegetative fertility, has obvious pagan overtones. The early church absorbed the pagan customs and traditions rather than attempt to totally destroy them. Pope Gregory declared to abbot Mellitus in AD 601 that he had given much thought to the conversion of the English and advised that their pagan temples should not be destroyed, but rather purified with holy water and Christian altars, which should be set up within them, instead of their pagan idols. Hundreds of years later, the tradition of the Green Man, one of those pagan idols that Pope Gregory had hoped to expunge, was still a powerful Celtic symbol of the old faith. In numerous ancient churches throughout Celtic Britain, these strange and often grotesque figures can be seen carved, often almost out of sight, on roof bosses, church bench ends and capitals.

Green Man
St Stephen's Church, Old Radnor, Powys

Now a sleepy backwater, Old Radnor today comprises not much more than a couple of houses, two or three farms, an excellent hostelry – The Harp Inn – and St Stephen's Church, built over the site of three Bronze Age earthworks.

The Green Man carved on to a capital in St Stephen's is but one of the links this ancient place has with its Celtic past. When the Normans came here they probably found a church already built and dedicated to a sixth-century Welsh saint, Ystyffan. Mistakenly they rededicated their new building to St Stephen, a popular Norman dedication. St Ystyffan was the first Christian martyr and was of royal blood, and his family ruled Powys from *c.* AD 600–850. Also in St Stephens church is a huge, roughly carved font sitting on four squat legs may well have been carved from a prehistoric standing stone. It has been dated to AD 800 or earlier and may well have once been used by St Ystyffan. Nearby are the 'Four Stones', a prehistoric grouping of megaliths that are said, according to legend, to represent four Welsh princes who died in battle. The stones mark their resting place, and each midsummer's night they are mysteriously covered in blood.

The Burry Man
South Queensferry, Edinburgh

In South Queensferry on the day before the annual Ferry Fair on the second Friday in August, an unusual custom takes place. No early written record of Burry Man is recorded in South Queensferry, but other herring fishing ports had their own Burry Man. Both in Buckie and in the Moray Firth records show that since at least the 1740s whenever the fishing was bad 'the fisherman would dress a copper in a flannel shirt with burrs stuck all over it, seat him in a hand-barrow, and wheel him in procession through the town, as a charm to raise the herring'. The South Queensferry procession is slightly different in that it seems to show gratitude for a good harvest, rather than being an attempt to cultivate one. It is plausible that the Burry Man was once a pagan fertility figure – a Green Man, not of the land but of the sea – and that his appearance before a fishing season got underway ensured a plentiful year.

The Gorsedd of Bards of the Isle of Britain
Bala, Gwynedd

The Gorsedd of Bards of the Isle of Britain, better known now as 'the Druids', is the inspiration of an eccentric eighteenth-century Welsh scholar, Iolo Morgannwg. He believed that the true descendants of the ancient Druids were the poets and musicians of Glamorgan, and that he himself was the last true Druid. To substantiate this, he forged a series of documents. In 1791, the first ceremony took place on Primrose Hill in London.

The history of the Eisteddfod dates back to Hywel Dda, a Welsh, tenth-century king, who is said to have given an honoured place in his household to an outstanding travelling poet. By the fifteenth century, the patronage these travelling poets and minstrels had enjoyed had all but disappeared and they were forced to perform in inns and taverns. Today the National Eisteddfod attracts more than 150,000 visitors, and entrants compete for prizes in the arts. It is held entirely in Europe's oldest living language – Welsh. However, no National Eisteddfod is complete without 'the Druids', who according to tradition must announce the coming of an Eisteddfod at least a year and a day prior to the event.

Cornish Gorsedd
Marazion, Cornwall

Each year at locations in Cornwall, the Gorseth Byrth Kernow (the Cornish Gorsedd ceremony) takes place. Cornish bards and new bards gather in their traditional blue robes, and process to a field where a huge circle is formed. Hymns are sung, the harp played and the initiation of new bards takes place. Local children add colour by performing a flower dance. Finally, with the sounding of the 'Horn of the Nation', the bards cry 'King Arthur is not dead'.

The Gorsedd was inaugurated in 1928 at Boscawen Un, by the Archdruid Pedrog of Wales. Although independent, it is allied to Druidic groups in Wales and Brittany. It exists to preserve the national Celtic spirit of Cornwall, to foster the study of Cornish history and the language, and also to promote Cornish literature and music.

Unlike Wales and Brittany, who are represented at the ceremony, Cornwall has neither Druids nor Ovates. The Gorsedd only confers the title of bard either in recognition of some manifestation of the Celtic spirit in work done for Cornwall, or for high proficiency in the Cornish language.

Bampton Morris Dancers and Bacup Coconut Dancers
Bampton, Oxfordshire and Bacup, Lancashire

The once traditional country dance of England was in decline until the folklorist Cecil Sharp recorded and revived it during the latter part of the nineteenth century. Morris dancers are now a familiar sight throughout the summer months. One of the first references to Morris dancing shows that it was clearly rooted in Britain as early as 1458, when Alice de Wetenhalle, the wife of a London merchant, presented a silver cup inscribed with the words 'cum moreys dance'. The origin of the name 'morris' was thought to have stemmed from 'Moorish', and to have come from North Africa or medieval Spain, brought by English soldiers returning from the Spanish wars in the fourteenth century. It may also have been introduced by Queen Eleanor of Castile, wife of Edward I, to her court. The theory being that the black face disguise personified the 'Moorish' people. There is no evidence to suggest that this type of dance was ever performed in either of these places. What we now call Morris dancing is probably the remnant of an ancient pre-Christian fertility dance. Traditionally performed in spring during Beltane (May Day), it undoubtedly has its origins in Celtic Britain.

Celtic Sun God Worship
Wiltshire

The Celts venerated divine forces along with water, and perhaps the most powerful of these gods was the sun god, Belenus. Neolithic and Bronze Age people aligned their funerary monuments with the moon and the sun. Archaeological evidence shows that since those prehistoric times man has worshipped and crafted symbols to idolize this life-giving force. Images of solar wheels and clay horses were votives to be cast into water by Iron Age people, and later certain dignitaries at Romano-Celtic sun cult observances wore solar ornamented headdresses.

The Celts celebrated the return of Belenus, who was considered a healer and a promoter of fertility, at Beltane, traditionally held on 1 May. Huge fires were lit across the country, and still are in Cornwall and Devon. Orgiastic festivals were held at ancient sacred sites to celebrate and draw magic from the sun.

The Angles Runway
St Merryn, Nr Padstow, Cornwall

The Angles Runway is a contemporary megalithic monument created in Edward Prynn's garden. Three huge granite block are topped by an enormous capstone, an almost exact larger-than-life copy of the Neolithic chamber tomb, Lanyon Quoit. It is one of many such monuments, all copies of more famous Cornish prehistoric sites. There is a huge stone circle, a rocking stone, a small version of the Men-an-Tol, and also the Tolvan Holed Stone. The Bronze Age original is at Gweek. This is the marriage stone, where Ed and his partner, Glynis, conduct 'Druid marriages'. Ed and Glynis are modern day Druids, tucked away in the tiny unspoiled and picturesque granite village of St Merryn, where they are pleased to welcome visitors to their Druidic garden.

Time Line

NEOLITHIC PERIOD

4,500 BC to 2,000 BC
Henge Monuments, Stone Circles, Monoliths

BRONZE AGE

2,000 BC to 750 BC
Stone Circles, Stone Rows, Round Barrows

IRON AGE

750 BC to AD 43
Hillforts, Celtic Hill Figures, Pictish culture, Druidism

ROMAN PERIOD

AD 43 to AD 476
AD 43 Roman Invasion of Britain
AD 50 Occupation of Wales
First missionaries arrive in Britain from Ireland and Continental
Europe to convert the British Celts

KING ARTHUR AND
THE AGE OF THE SAINTS

AD 476 to AD 1066
End of fifth century: birth of King Arthur
AD 537 Battle of Camlann, King Arthur dies. Transported to Glastonbury
AD 563 Irish Evangelist St Columba founds monastery on Iona, Scotland
AD 596 Pope Gregory sends Augustine prior of his own monastery of
   St Andrew to convert the heathen English. Spectacularly successful, 10,000
   of the English were baptized on Christmas Day
AD 664 Synod of Whitby
AD 793 Vikings sack the monastery on Lindisfarne, Northumbria
AD 1016 Danish King Canute, King of all England and part of Scotland

MEDIEVAL PERIOD

AD 1066 to AD 1500
Celtic Carvings in Churches
AD 1492 Columbus reaches America

CONTEMPORARY CELTS

AD 1500 to Present
Neo-Drudism

BIBLIOGRAPHY

Anderson, William and Hicks, Clive, *Green Man* (HarperCollins, 1990)

Ashwell, K. Y., *St Germoe Church* (Cornwall, 1995)

Barber, Chris, *Mysterious Wales* (David & Charles, 1982)

Barber, Chris, *More Mysterious Wales* (Paladin, 1987)

Barber, Chris, and Williams, John G., *The Ancient Stones of Wales* (Blorenge Books, 1989)

Berresford, Ellis Peter, *A Guide to Early Celtic Remains in Britain* (Constable, 1991)

Betty, J. H., and Taylor, C. W. G., *Sacred and Static Mediaeval Stone Carving in the West Country* (Redcliffe Press, 1982)

Bond, Francis, *Fonts and Font Covers* (OUP, 1908)

Bord, Janet and Colin, *Ancient Mysteries of Britain* (Diamond Books, 1991)

Bord, Janet and Colin, *Earth Rites* (Granta, 1982)

Bord, Janet and Colin, *Sacred Waters* (Granta, 1985)

Burl, Aubrey, *Prehistoric Stone Circles* (Shire Publications, 1979)

Burl, Aubrey, *Rites of the Gods* (Dent and Sons Ltd, 1981)

Burl, Aubrey, *The Stone Circles of the British Isles* (Yale University Press, 1989)

Children, George and Nash, George, *Prehistoric Sites of Herefordshire* (Logaston Press, 1994)

Christian, Roy, *Old English Customs* (Country Life Ltd, 1966)

Christian, Roy, *Well-Dressing in Derbyshire* (Derbyshire Countryside Ltd, 1991)

Christie, Patricia, *Chysauster and Carn Euny* (English Heritage, 1993)

Clifton-Taylor, Alec, *English Parish Churches as Works of Art* (Batsford 1974)

Coghlan, Ronan, *The Encyclopaedia of Arthurian Legends* (Element Books, 1991)

Cooke, Ian, *Mermaid to Merrymaid: Journey to the Stones* (Men-an-Tol Studio, 1987)

David, Christopher Rev., *St Winefride's Well: A History and Guide* (1990)

Delaney, Frank, *The Celts* (HarperCollins, 1993)

Delap, Dana, *Celtic Saints* (The Pitkin Guide, 1995)

Derrick, Freda, *Tales Told in Church Stone* (Lutterworth Press, 1935)

English Heritage, *Ceremonies of the Gorsedd of the Bards of Cornwall*

Fairhurst, Horace, *Exploring Arran's Past*, (Kilbrannan Publishing, 1988)

Fojut, Noel, *Prehistoric and Viking Shetland* (Shetland Times, 1994)

Green, Miranda, *Dictionary of Celtic Myths and Legends* (Thames & Hudson, 1992)

Gregory, Donald, *Wales Before 1066 – A Guide* (Gwasg Carreg Gwalch, 1989)

Hadingham, Evan, *Circles and Standing Stones* (Heinemann, 1975)

Hayward, John, *Dartmoor 365* (Curlew Publications, 1991)

Hogg, A. H. A., *Hill Forts of Britain* (Hart-Davis MacGibbon, 1975)

Iona Community, *Iona Abbey and Nunnery Official Guide Book* (Iona Abbey Ltd)

Jenkins, Elizabeth, *The Mysteries of King Arthur* (Michael Joseph, 1975)

Jones, Margaret, *Eisteddfod – A Welsh Phenomenon*, (1986)

Jones, Sally, *Legends of Devon* (Bossiney Books, 1981)

Kelly, L. V., *Saint Illtud's Church* (D Brown and Sons, 1993)

Knightly, Charles, *The Customs and Ceremonies of Britain* (Thames & Hudson, 1986)

Laing, Lloyd, *Celtic Britain: Britain before the Conquest* (Routledge and Kegan Paul, 1979)

Macinnes, Lesley, *Anglesey, A Guide to Ancient and Historic Sites on the Isle of Anglesey* (Cadw, 1989).

Norton-Taylor, Duncan, *The Celts: The Emergence of Man* (Time Life International, 1975)

Parishioners of Meifod, *The History of the Church of St Tysilio and St Mary Meifod*

Pegg, John, *After Dark on Dartmoor* (John Pegg Publishing, 1985)

Pegg, John, *The Face of Dartmoor* (John Pegg Publishing, 1985)

Pepin, David, *Discovering Shrines and Holy Places* (Shire Publications, 1980)

Rees, Nona, *St Davids of Dewisland* (Gomer Press, 1996)

Roberts, Jack, *The Sheela-Na-Gigs of Britain and Ireland* (Banda Publishing, Ireland)

Roberts, Tomos, *Eglwys Llangwyfan Yn y Mok* (Ritchie Graham and Harman, Mary, *Exploring Scotland's Heritage* HMSO Edinburgh, 1986)

Ritchie, Anna, and Breeze, David J., *Invaders of Scotland*, (HMSO Edinburgh, 1991)

Ross, Stewart, *Ancient Scotland* (Lochar Publishing, 1991)

Senior, Michael, *Anglesey, The Island's Story* (Gwasg Carreg Gwalch, 1996)

Shuel, Brian, *The National Trust Guide to Traditional Customs of Britain* (Webb and Bower, 1985)

Simpson, Douglas, *Dunnottar Castle* The Estate Office, Dunecht, 1926/1993)

Smith, J. C. D., *Church Wood Carvings, A West Country Study* (David & Charles, 1969)

Stanford, S. C., *The Malvern Hillforts: Midsummer Hill and the British Camp*, (Malvern Hill Conservators, 1988)

Sykes, Homer, *Once a Year, some Traditional British Customs* (Gordon Fraser, 1977)

Sykes, Homer, *Mysterious Britain* (Weidenfeld & Nicolson, 1993)

Terry, John, *Sacred Stones* (Gomer Press, 1994)

Thomas, Charles, *Celtic Britain* (Thames & Hudson, 1986)

Thomas, Charles, *Tintagel Castle* (English Heritage, 1995)

Toulson, Shirley, *Celtic Journeys in Scotland and the North of England* (Fount, 1995)

Watts, Kenneth, *The Marlborough Downs* (Ex Libris Press, 1993)

Weatherhill, Craig, *Cornovia, Ancient Sites of Cornwall and Scilly* (Alison Hodge, 1985)

The Welsh Water Authority, *Archaeological Excavations Brenig*

Williams, Michael, *Strange Happenings in Cornwall* (Bossiney Books, 1981)

Wright, Peter Poyntz, *The Rural Bench Ends of Somerset* (Avebury Publishing, 1983)

Wyn, Evans J., *St David's Cathedral*, (A Pitkin Cathedral Guide, 1994)

INDEX

Page numbers in *italics* indicate illustrations

Author's Notes and Acknowledgements

This is the third book I have produced for the Country Series and the second that I have photographed and written. It has been a privilege to work on this project and to have almost complete control. Any mistakes are mine.

This volume offered me the freedom once again to explore the remarkable landscape of Celtic Britain, to revisit and discover places I had only read about. I shall never forget in the late summer sunlight when I was at St Cwyfan's Church, near Aberffaw, watching a sparrow-hawk hunt, while whinchats circled and grouped before setting off for warmer winter sunshine, and two sandwich terns with yellow distinguishing flashes on their long beaks stood on a rock watching a group of more than twenty ramblers from Bradford eat their picnics. It seemed at the time incredible that there was anyone at all at this tranquil and isolated place. Happy childhood memories came flooding back when I was at St Davids, of a camping holiday with my aunt Flo and uncle Con and their family. The rugged beauty, precariously steep cliffs leading to quiet sheltered bays of white sand. I enjoyed my first sea-fishing experience here. I can recall buying small, round lead weights, and stringing them necklace-like on to the catgut line. I remember the colourful red and yellow float, and also how proud I was of the larger lead weight, lifebelt-like, with small round protruding nodes forming a circle around the top surface. Happy recollections of crabbing and collecting winkles, and then sitting in the lee of my aunt's tent while handfulls of these small, almost black shellfish were put into a pan of water and brought to the boil over a primus stove. Then being shown how to delicately pick out this fish meat, by peeling off the black, flat, farthing-sized 'head' and, with a bent pin, picking out the delicious coiled meat.

I used a Mamiya RZ67 for nearly all the landscape photographs. I do so enjoy the slow and controlled method of working that this Mamiya forces on one. I worked through 6,000 years, in six months of 1996, reading many books and compiling information that I found interesting. I am principally a photographer, and what I have learned has been gleaned very often from scholars who may well have spent years, if not their professional lives, investigating very specific periods covered in this volume. I am indebted to their thorough and continuing work. The books mentioned in the Bibliography may well be of interest to readers who want more detailed information. I can particularly recommend the books by Dr Aubrey Burl, who writes with the greatest authority, accuracy, and in a readable way that brings his subject back to life. I should also like to thank Cliff Osenton who explained to me how he believes our prehistoric ancestors built many of the monuments in this book and how and why he came to those conclusions.

I would like to thank Geoff Howard for his friendship, support and technical assistance, Peter Baistow and Peter Jordan for their friendship and support while I worked on this project, and my colleagues at Network Photographers. My thanks also go to Hywel Wyn Edwards, of the National Eisteddfod, Bala; J. G. Edwards, the former rector of St Anne's church, Whitstone; The Rev. Andrew T. Greaves of St Fergus's Kirk, Glamis; Historic Scotland; Canon David Jenkins of Llanwit Major Parish Church; A. Euros Jones of The Countryside Management Service, Aberffraw, Anglesey, for giving up valuable time; and Paul Gatt and his team at Push One in Chelsea, who once again processed all of my film with great speed, efficiency, and with a smile, often burning the midnight oil on my behalf. All the photographs in this book were taken on Kodak film. Their new films have tremendous colour saturation, fine grain and are a joy to use. Additional thanks to Father Bernard Lordan, of St Winefride's Church, Holywell; The Royal Commission on the Ancient and Historical Monuments of Scotland, who kindly supplied me with details on various sites 'derived from information compiled and which is the copyright of RCAHMS'; The Malvern Hill Conservators; The Vaughan family, Huntsham Court, Near Symonds Yat; and Lee Filters of Andover, Hampshire – I have made extensive use of their excellent filter system. In all the medium format landscape photographs I used a combination of their subtle colour enhancing filters. Finally, thanks to Beth Vaughan at Weidenfeld & Nicolson who managed the project, and for her patience as deadlines loomed ever closer. My thanks go principally to Michael Dover for commissioning this volume and allowing me to get on with it.